Longman Test Practice Kits

Mathematics

Key Stage 1

Brian Speed • Linda Terry

LONGMAN

LONGMAN TEST PRACTICE KITS

Series editors
Geoff Black and Stuart Wall

Titles available

Key Stage 1	*Key Stage 2*	*Key Stage 3*
English	English	English
Mathematics	Mathematics	Mathematics
Mental Maths Tests	Mental Maths Tests	Mental Maths Tests
	Science	Science

Pearson Education Limited
Edinburgh Gate, Harlow
Essex, CM20 2JE England
and Associated Companies throughout the world

Visit our website at *www.awl-he.com/studyguides*

© Addison Wesley Longman 1999

The right of Brian Speed and Linda Terry to be identified as authors of this work has been asserted by them in accordance with the Copyright, Designs and Patents Act 1988

All rights reserved; no part of this publication may be reproduced, stored in any retrieval system, or transmitted in any form or by any means, electronic, mechanical, photocopying, recording, or otherwise without either the prior written permission of the Publishers or a licence permitting restricted copying in the United Kingdom issued by the Copyright Licensing Agency Ltd., 90 Tottenham Court Road, London W1P 0LP.

First published 1999
Third impression 1999

British Library Cataloguing in Publication Data
A catalogue entry for this title is available from the British Library

ISBN 0-582-41490-3

Set by 32 in Futura, Frutiger Light and Bauer Bodoni
Printed in Singapore (KKP)

Table of contents

The Key Stage 1 National Tests   vi
Mathematics at Key Stage 1   vi
Levels of achievement   vi

Using this book   vii
Helping your child to improve   vii

Part 1 – Test practice papers   1
Administering the tests   1
Test A   2
Test B   17
Test C   31

Part 2 – Answers   42
Marking the tests   42
Answers to Test A   43
Answers to Test B   50
Answers to Test C   57
Marking grid   62

The Key Stage 1 National Tests

During the first two years at school your child will cover Key Stage 1 of the National Curriculum. Towards the end of Year 2 (at age 7) he or she will take the National Curriculum Tests in Mathematics and English (often referred to as SATs). These written tests are taken in your child's own school and are carried out under the supervision of their own teachers. They are marked within the school, but external moderators will then check the marks to make sure that the same standards have been applied in all schools.

Mathematics at Key Stage 1

The National Curriculum divides Mathematics at Key Stage 1 into three sections called Attainment Targets (ATs).

AT1   Using and Applying Mathematics
AT2   Number
AT3   Shape, Space and Measures

AT1, Using and Applying Mathematics, is assessed by your child's teacher through normal classroom activity. It is the other two ATs (AT2 and AT3) that are assessed in the National Tests. Children working at Level 1 in Mathematics will usually undertake practical mathematical tasks under the supervision of their teacher. Children who are assessed by their teacher to be working beyond Level 1 will take a written test, usually in May of Year 2.

The results of the written National Tests for Key Stage 1 Mathematics will be available to you, as parents, by the end of July of Year 2 (age 7). Your child's results will be expressed as a level for each subject assessed. As well as the level for the written tests in Mathematics, you will also receive the results of the classroom assessments made by your child's teacher of work undertaken during the year (called 'Teacher Assessment').

You will also receive a summary of the Key Stage 1 results in Mathematics achieved by all the other students in your school, and for all students nationally. You will then be able to check your child's progress against other students of the same age.

Levels of achievement

At Key Stage 1 each subject is divided into Levels 1 to 3. By the end of Year 2 (age 7), most children should be working at Levels 1 to 3, although in some cases children may still be said to be 'working towards' Level 1.

On average, most children will achieve Level 2 by the end of Year 2 (age 7) and a few will reach Level 3. Only very rarely will a child achieve Level 4.

The table below illustrates the percentage of students (nationally) who are expected to achieve each level. Clearly most children achieve one of the 'bands' of Level 2.

Level	Percentage
1	15
2C At the threshold of Level 2	20
2B In the middle of Level 2	25
2A Towards the top of Level 2	30
3	10

Using this book

- The tests in this book have been designed to help children aged 6 or 7 prepare for the written Mathematics Test at Key Stage 1.
- The tests cover Levels 2 and 3 of the National Curriculum.
- If your child experiences difficulty in answering the questions at the beginning of a test, then they may not be ready to tackle work at that Level just yet.
- Encourage your child to go back at the end of the test to check their answers and perhaps *attempt any questions not answered*.
- After the test has been completed, check your child's answers. There are answers with examiner hints for each Test Paper at the back of the book.
- Remember to fill in the marking grid and to check the Level achieved. Of course the Levels given are intended only as an indication of how your child has performed on this test. Further practice can improve their level of achievement.

Helping your child to improve

To improve your child's score it may help to go back over the test with them:

- Identify any questions that have not been attempted or in which an error has been made.
- Talk about the *reason* why that question was missed or a mistake was made. Was it due to a misunderstanding of the question? Was it due to an error in calculation? Was it due to a lack of time to think about the problem?
- Look at the questions together. Pick out the key words or ideas in that question so that your child can more readily identify what is required.
- Let your child try the question again and check whether they can get the correct answer once they have understood the question. Examiner hints alongside the answers might help here.

If the reason for an error seems to be a lack of time, then remember the following:

- In the actual test your child will have in school, there is no specific time limit; the teacher will try to assess how long the *whole group* needs and will not move on to the next question until reasonably sure that all the group have been able to have a go at the question, or that they simply couldn't do it (however long they had!).
- Your child can try the other timed tests in this book. Practice really does help a child get used to working in a given time.

PART 1
Test practice papers

Administering the tests

- Each of the tests should take your child about 45 minutes to complete, but allow more time if you feel they wish to continue and are able to complete it.
- Make sure that your child has pencils, a rubber, a ruler and access to a small mirror (if needed for a reflection question).
- Tell your child that you can give some help if they cannot read the words of a question, but that you cannot help by showing how to do a problem.
- Explain that the space around the questions may be used for working out answers (unless you wish to provide additional sheets of paper), but that the answer should be written on the pages of the book, as indicated for each question.
- Ensure that your child understands that many of the questions have diagrams or pictures which may help in finding the correct answer.
- Explain that the questions may become more difficult as they work through the questions, and if one question is difficult it is better not to worry, but to leave that question and move on to the next one.
- In the National Test, the first five questions are *read* to the children by the teacher. Although they are printed in this book, if you wish to make the practice test exactly like the actual test, then these questions (1–5) may be read out to your child.

MATHEMATICS
Test A

1 What is the next number?

8   10   12   14

2 Write the number **twenty six** in figures.

3 What is the **total cost** of the banana and the apple?

Banana 10p

Apple 7p

☐ p

4 Tick all the **triangles** in the box.

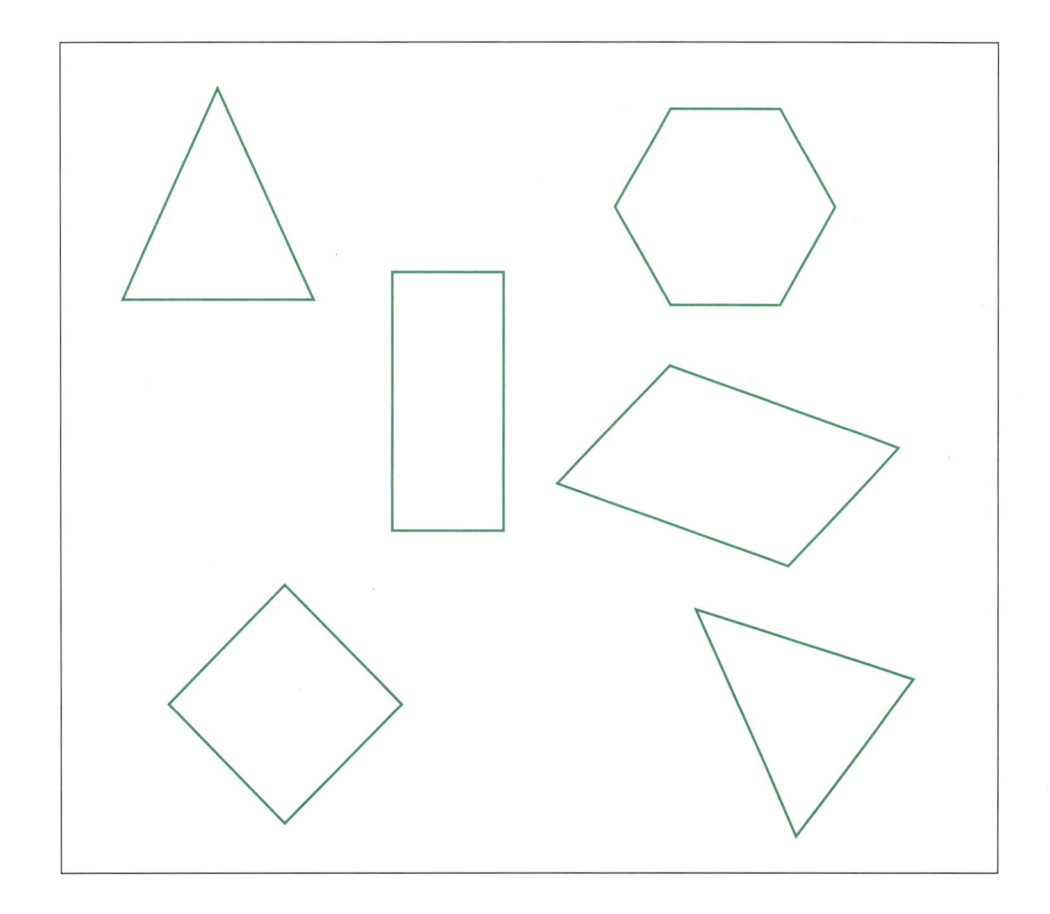

5 One of these sums has the answer **8**.
Draw a ring round the sum which has an answer of **8**.

$$3 + 4 \qquad 9 - 2$$

$$10 - 2 \qquad 5 + 4$$

6 Write in the missing numbers.

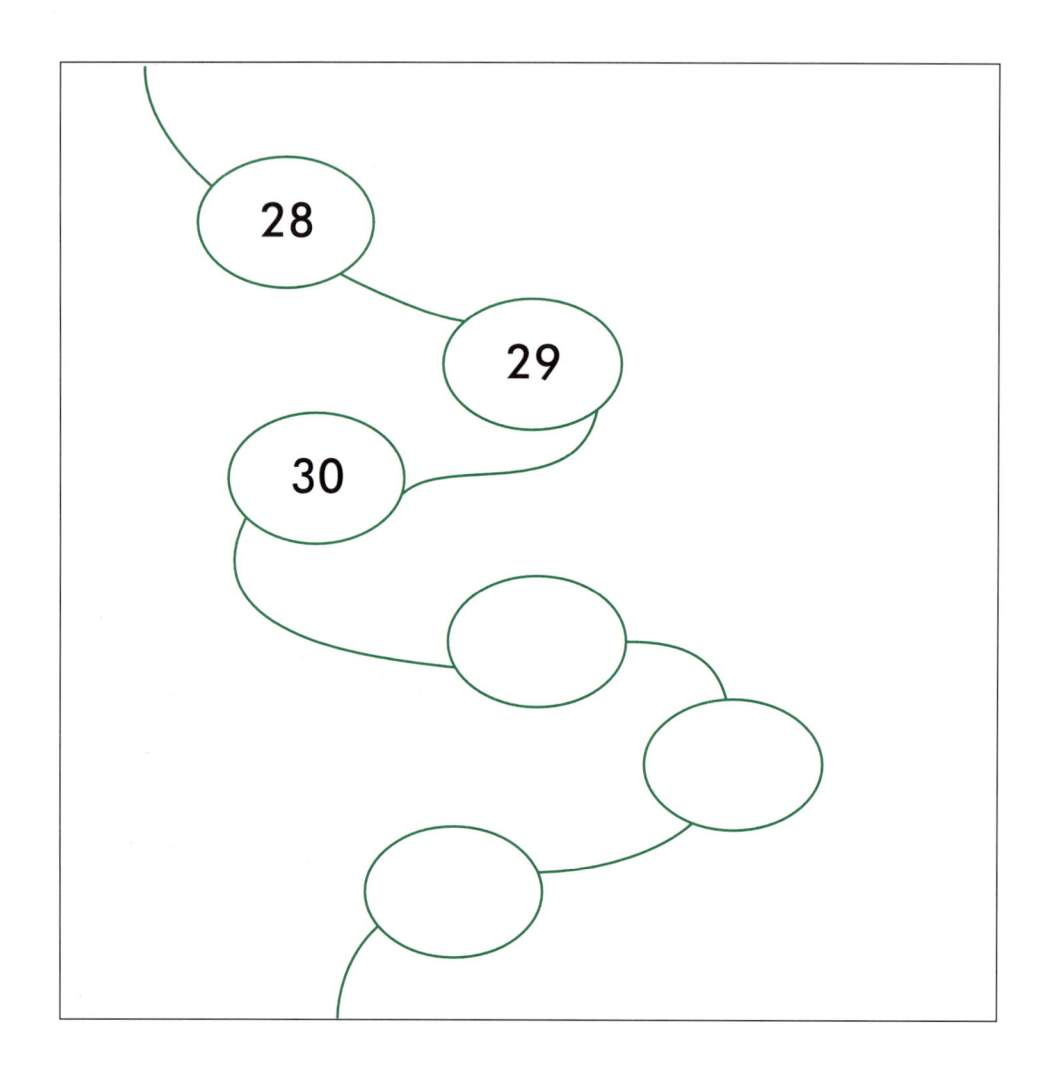

[diagram showing a chain of ovals connected by a line: 28, 29, 30, and three empty ovals]

7 Draw a ring around the **even** numbers.

16   9   31   18

50   28   23

8 Draw a ring around **half** of the apples.

9 Put a tick by the line which is **4** centimetres long.

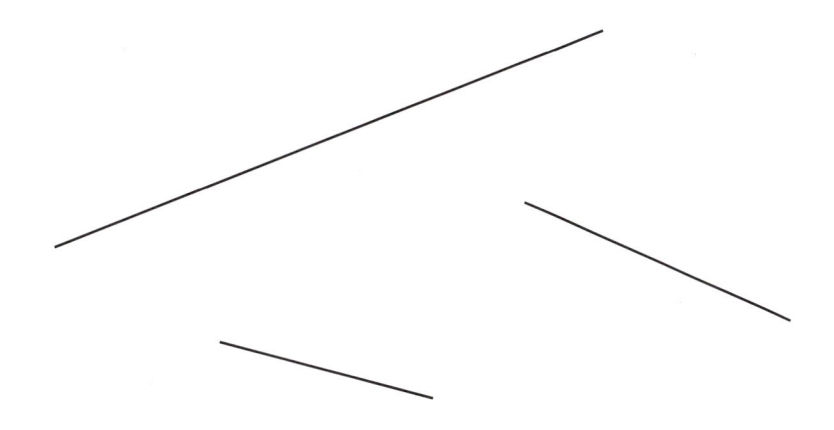

10 What time does the clock show?

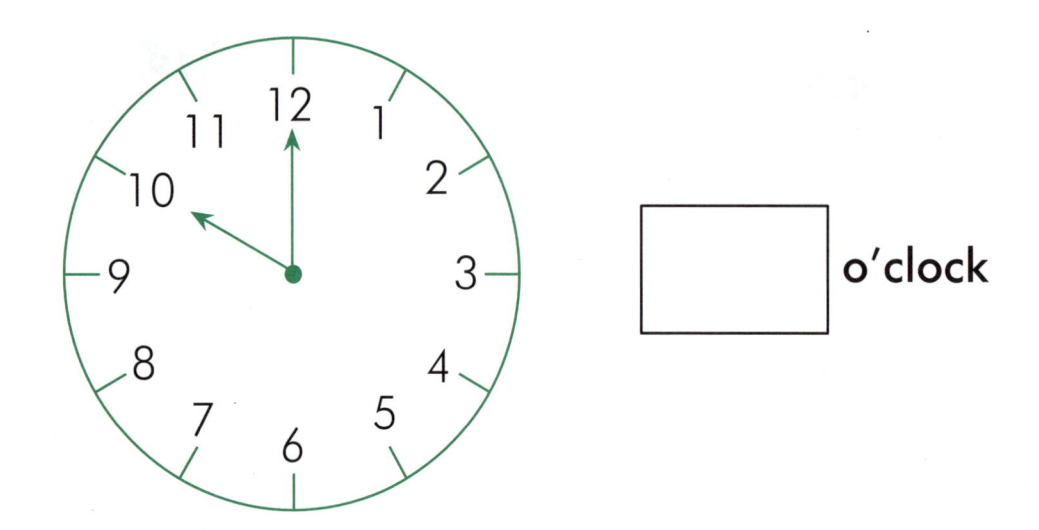

☐ o'clock

11 Put a cross (×) in all the shapes with **right angles**.

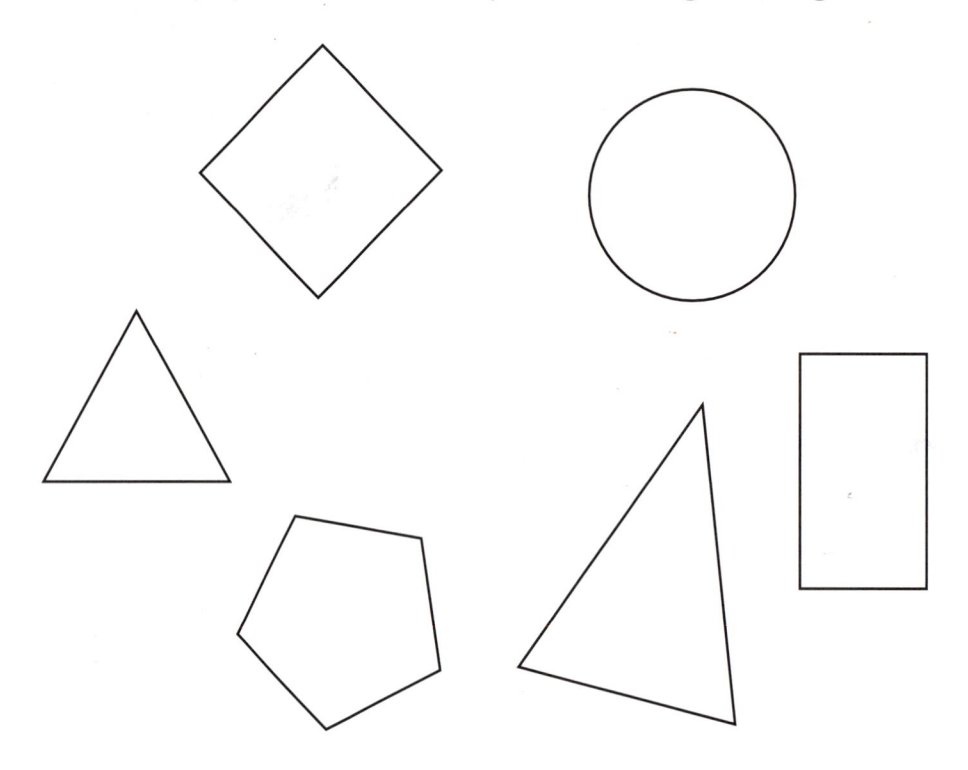

12 How much money is in the purse?

☐ pence

13 Write numbers in the shapes to add up to **11**.

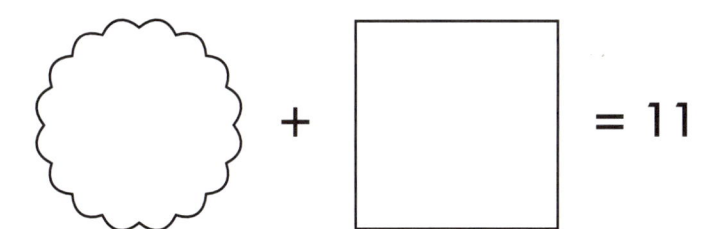

◯ + ☐ = 11

14 Some children chose their favourite colour.
They drew a **pictogram**.

Favourite colours

Number of children

Red: 3 faces
Blue: 5 faces
Yellow: 4 faces
Green: (empty)

☺ means 1 child

Colours

(a) Two children liked green best.
Show this on the pictogram.

(b) More children liked blue than red.
How many more?

☐ children

15 Look at these three number cards.

3   7   4

Use **two** of these cards to make a number which is less than **70**.
Write one number in each card.

16 Join each sum to its answer on the line.

6   7   8   9   10   11   12   13

(6 + 5)   (7 + 6)

(9 − 2)

17 What is the **total** number of dots?

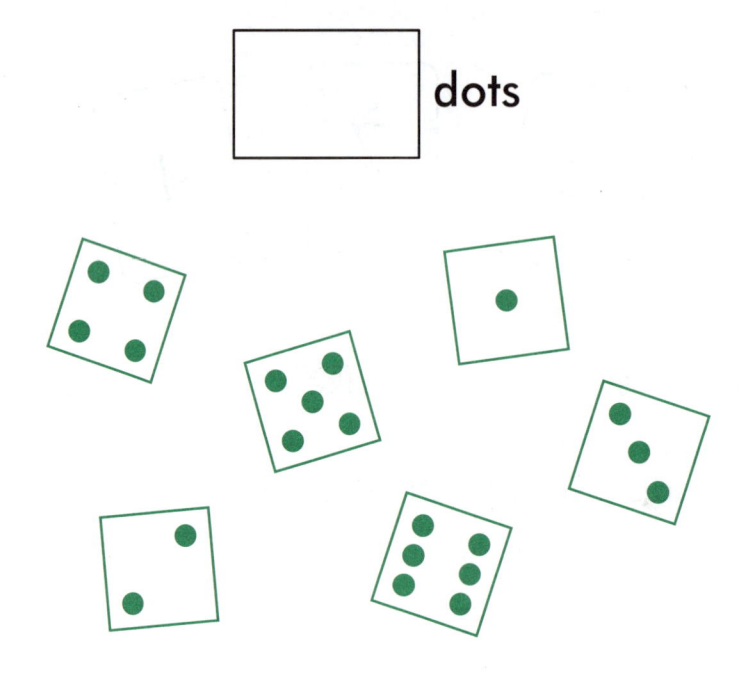

☐ dots

18 Write these numbers in order. Start with the smallest number.

52   123   85   117

232   198

☐ ☐ ☐ ☐ ☐ ☐
smallest

19 Continue this number pattern.
Fill in the missing numbers.

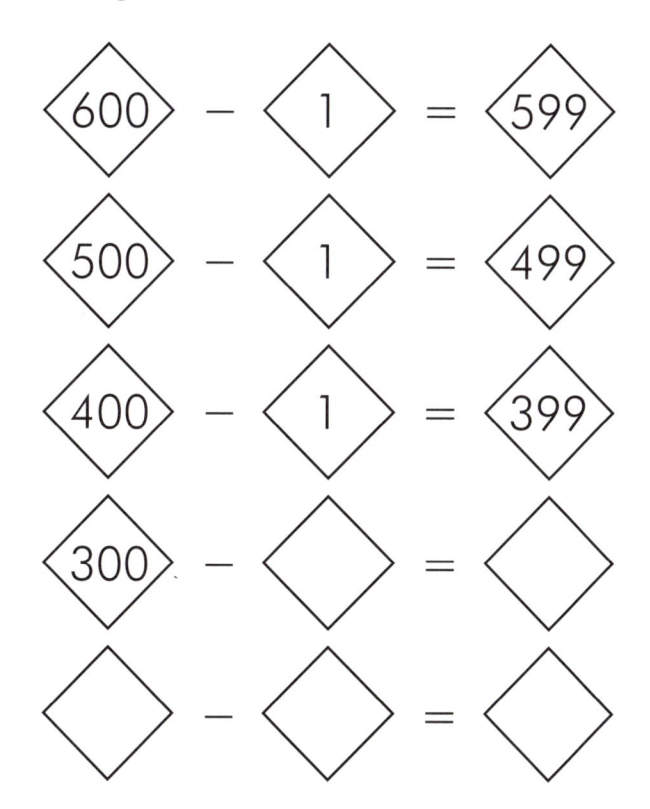

600 − 1 = 599

500 − 1 = 499

400 − 1 = 399

300 − ☐ = ☐

☐ − ☐ = ☐

20 This clock shows when it stopped raining.

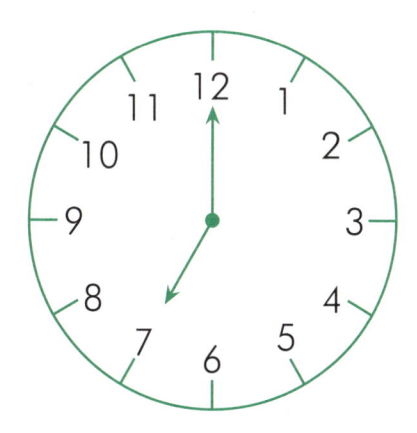

It started raining **2** hours earlier.
What time did it start raining?

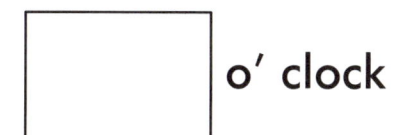

☐ o' clock

21 Find the answer.

$$52 - 17 = \boxed{}$$

22 Ice creams cost **65p**.

Mary has **50p**.
How much more does Mary need to be able to buy the ice cream?

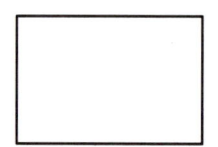

$\boxed{}$

23 Draw the reflection of this shape.

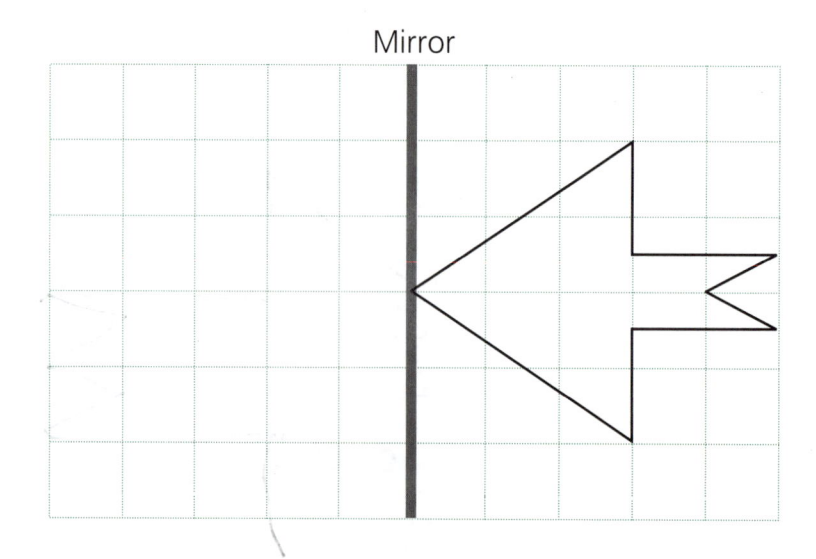

Mirror

24

	Less than 30	More than 30
Odd numbers	5	
Even numbers		126

Put these numbers in the correct places on the diagram.

(a) **12** and **139**
(b) **17** and **152**

25 This chart shows the number of hours that the sun shone in one week.

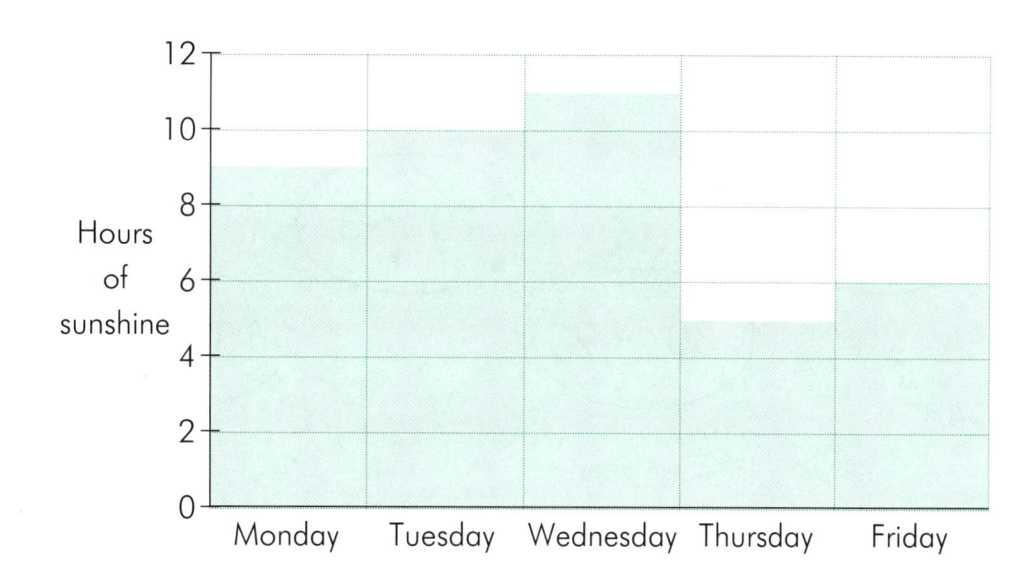

(a) Which day was the sunniest?

(b) Which day had **9** hours of sunshine?

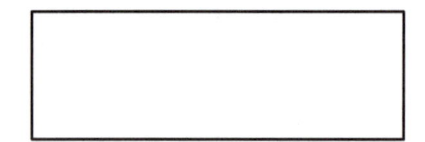

(c) How many hours of sunshine were there on **Thursday**?

☐ hours

26 Write the answer to the sum.

77 + 35 = ☐

27 Join each sum to its answer.

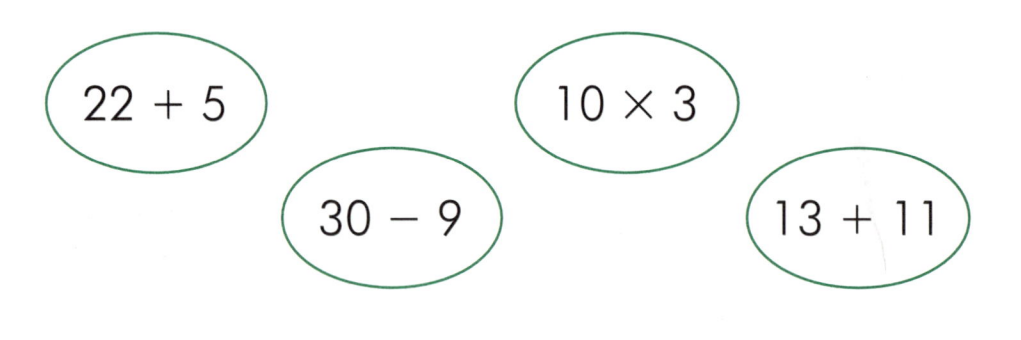

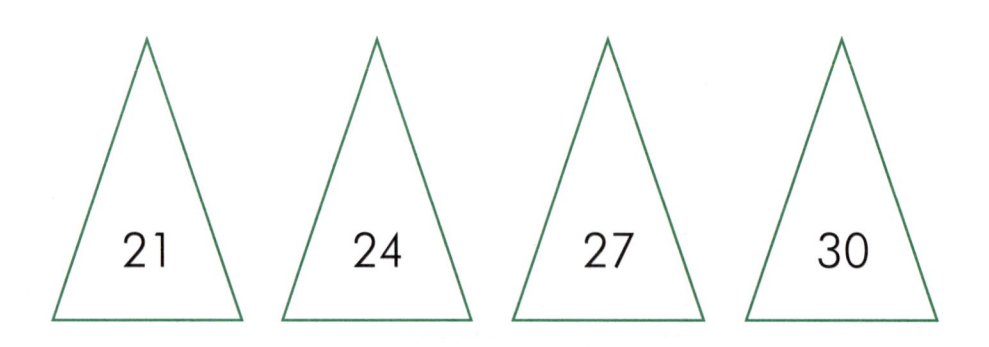

22 + 5   10 × 3

  30 − 9   13 + 11

21   24   27   30

28 Put a number in the box to make this sum correct.

$$200 = \boxed{} + 138$$

29 Which number is the arrow pointing to? Write the number in the box.

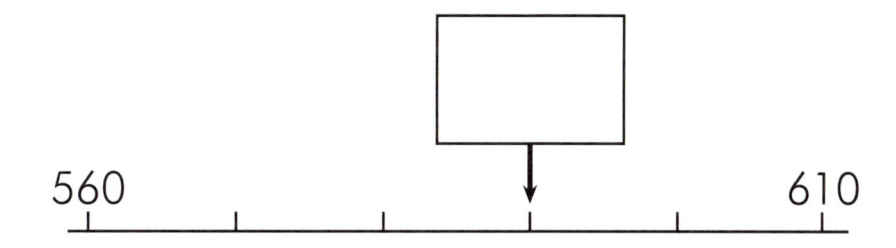

560 ↓ 610

30 Write the name underneath each shape.

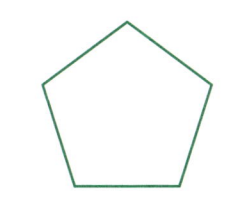

_____   _____

_____   _____

31 Mary has a party.
There are **18** children at the party.
There are **12** girls.
How many boys are there at the party?

☐ boys

32 Some of these numbers can be divided **exactly by 5**.
Draw a ring around the numbers that can be divided **exactly by 5**.

25   13

50   30   16

39   100

MATHEMATICS

Test B

1 Write the number **fifty eight** in figures in the box.

2 Put a tick (✓) in the **square**.

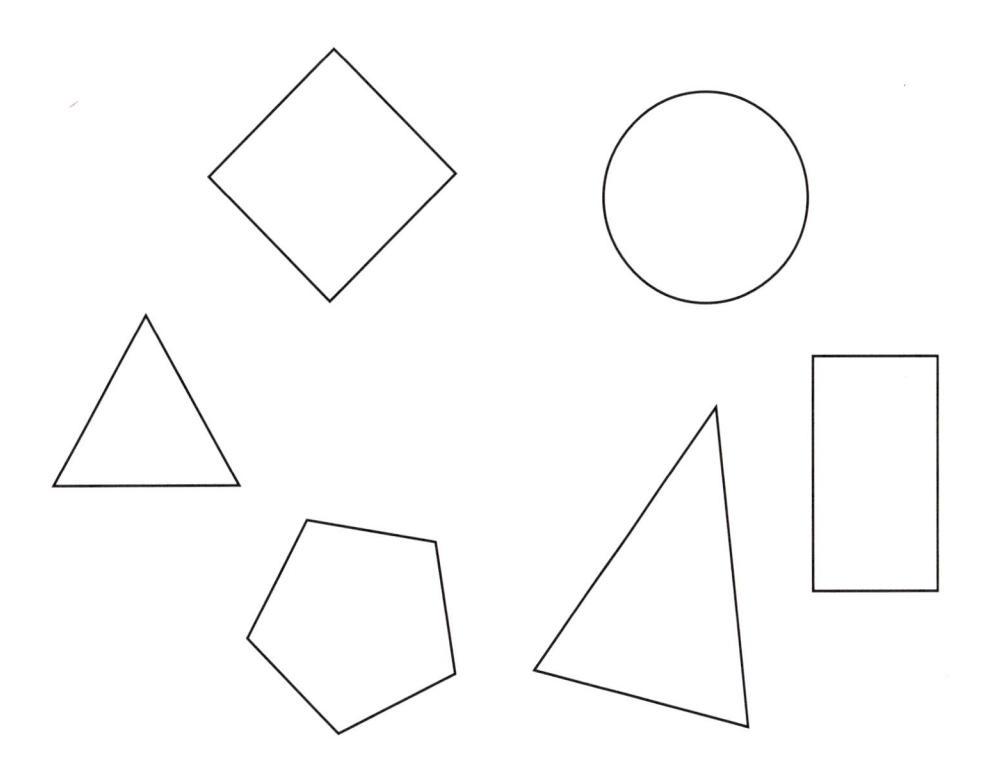

3 What is the total of **three** and **eight**?

4 How much money is there altogether?

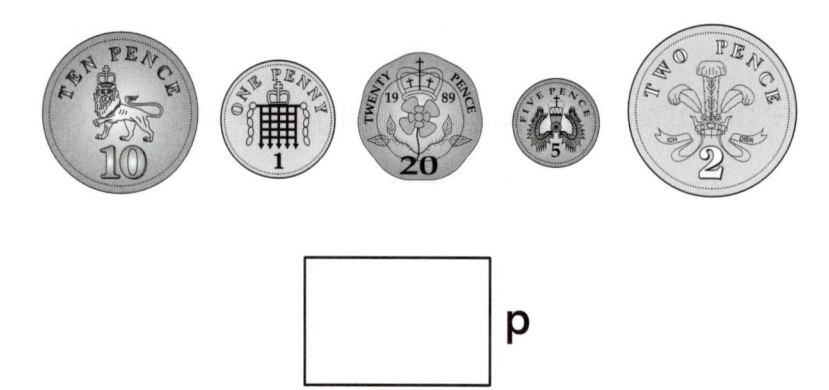

☐ p

5 Draw a ring around the **smallest** number.

6   14   3   7   12

6 Fill in the **missing** number.

4 + ☐ = 9

7 Join each shape to its name.

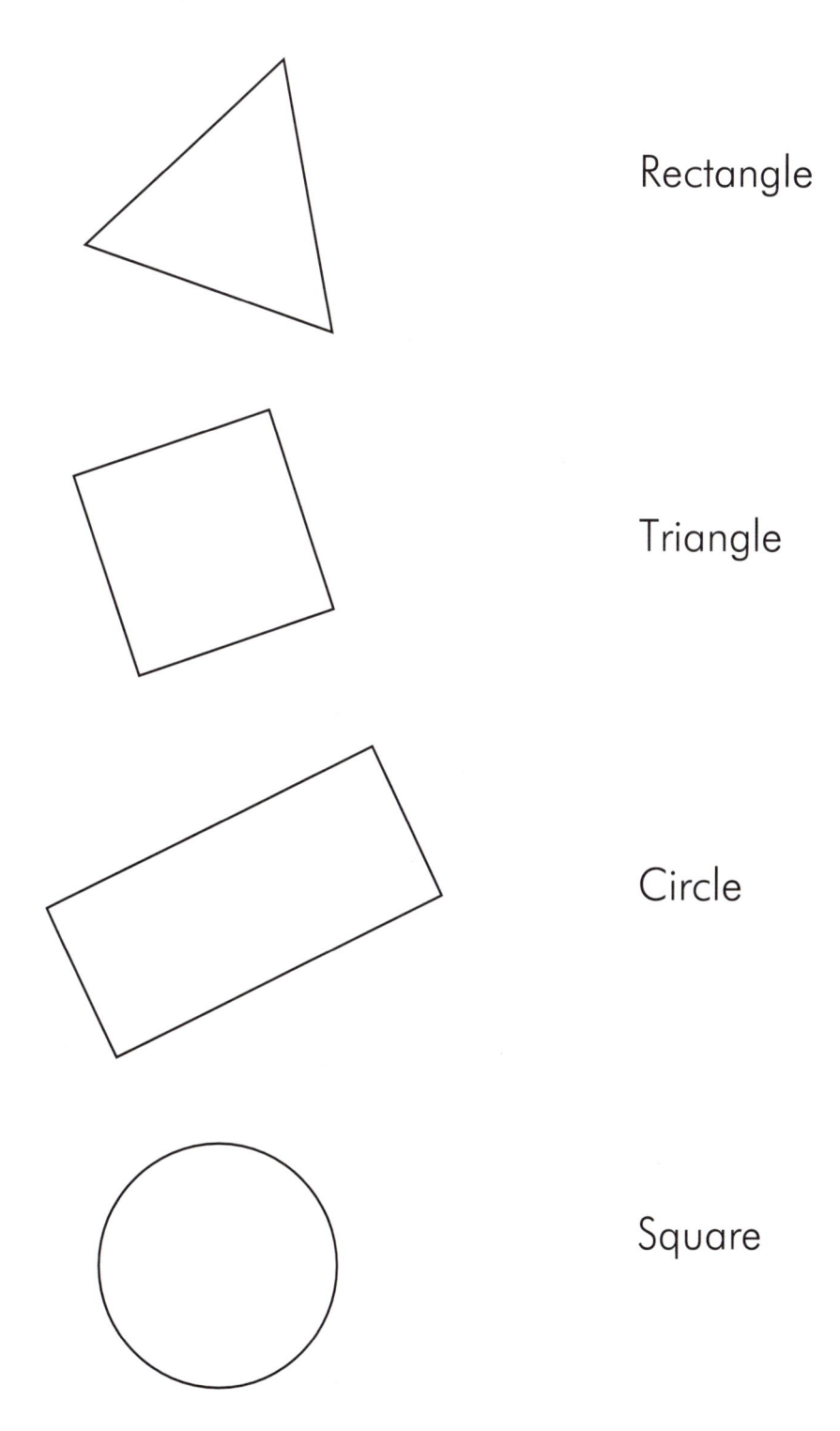

Rectangle

Triangle

Circle

Square

8 Colour **half** of the flowers.

9 Join each picture to the word used to **measure** it.

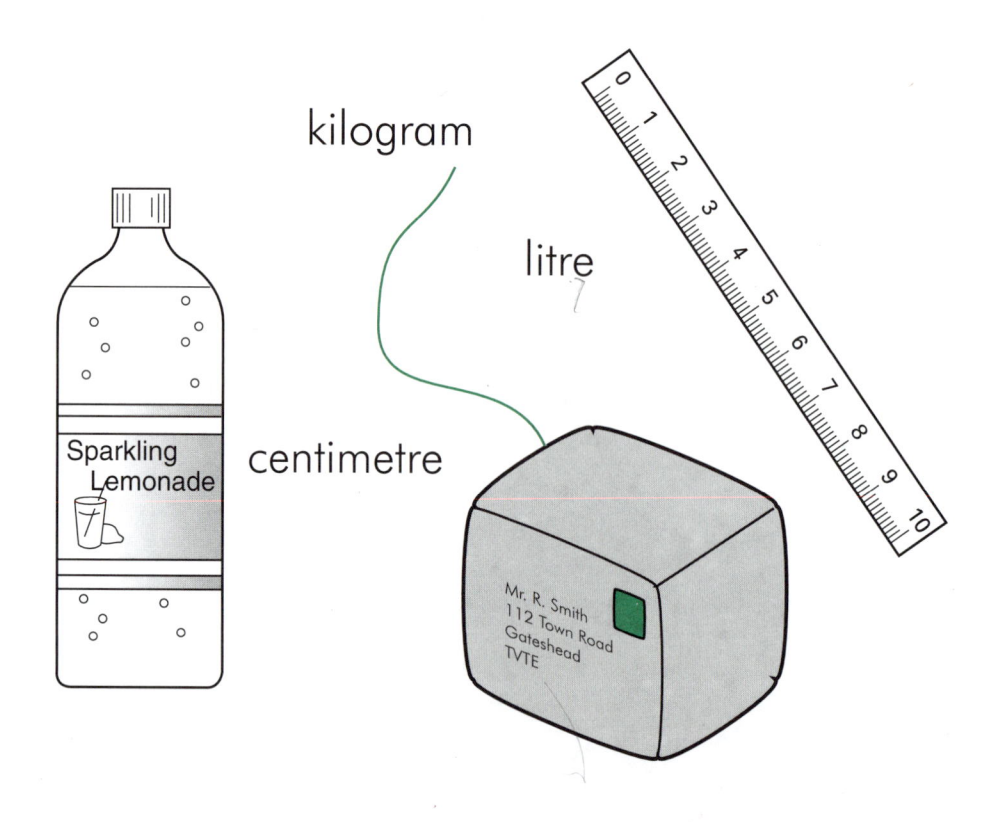

kilogram

litre

centimetre

10 This shape has turned through one **right angle**.

Tick (✓) the boxes where the shape has turned through one **right angle**.

11 Write three **odd** numbers less than **20**.

12 This cake cost **10p**.

How many cakes can you buy with **50p**?

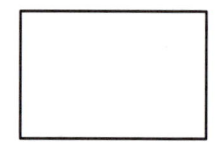

☐

13 Write these numbers **in order**. Start with the smallest number.

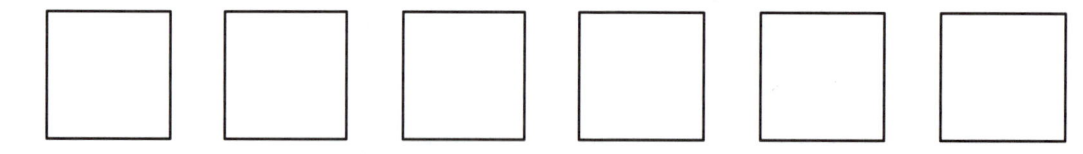

61   16   92

29   35   5

☐ ☐ ☐ ☐ ☐ ☐
smallest

14 These children have pets.

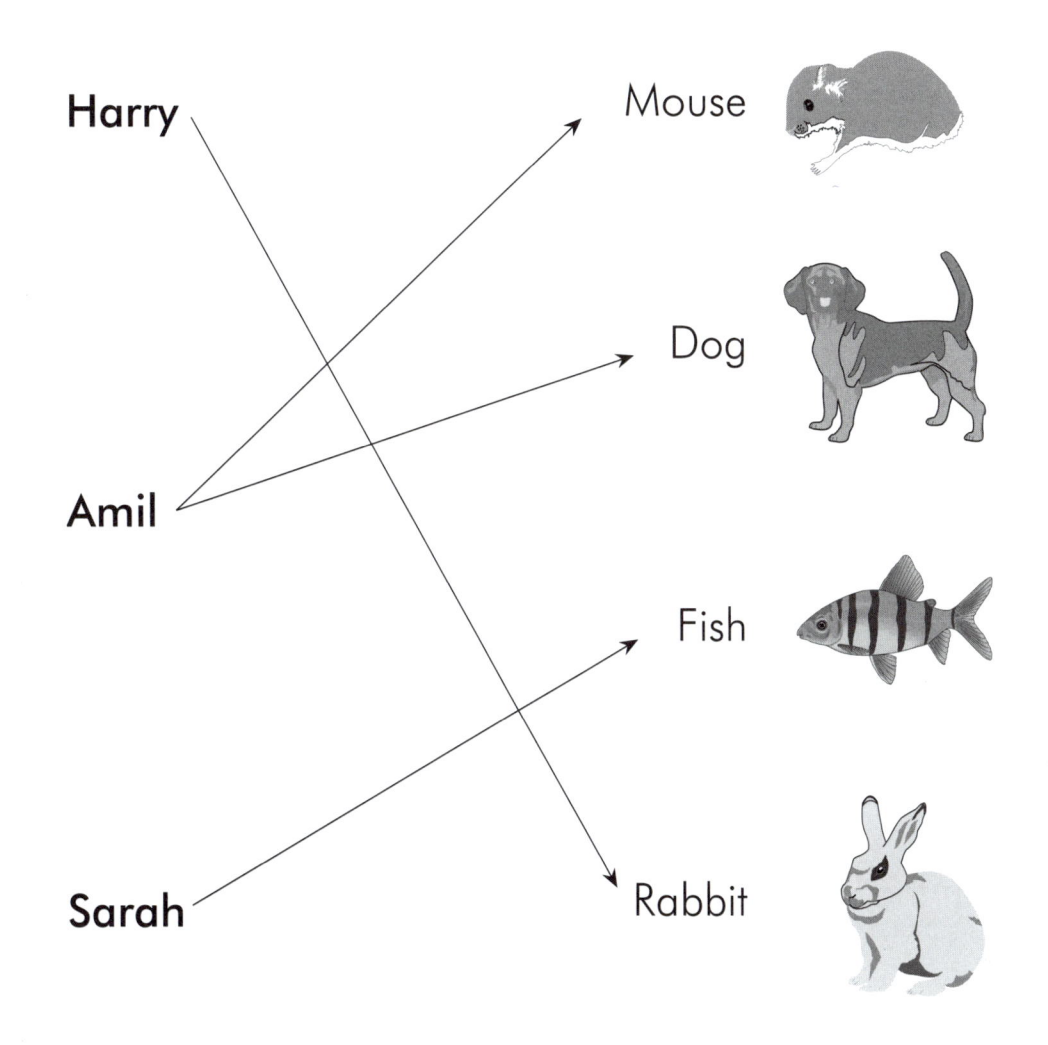

Harry → Fish

Amil → Mouse
Amil → Rabbit

Sarah → Dog

(a) Who has **2** pets?

(b) Who has a **rabbit**?

15 Draw lines to match **12** to two of these boxes.

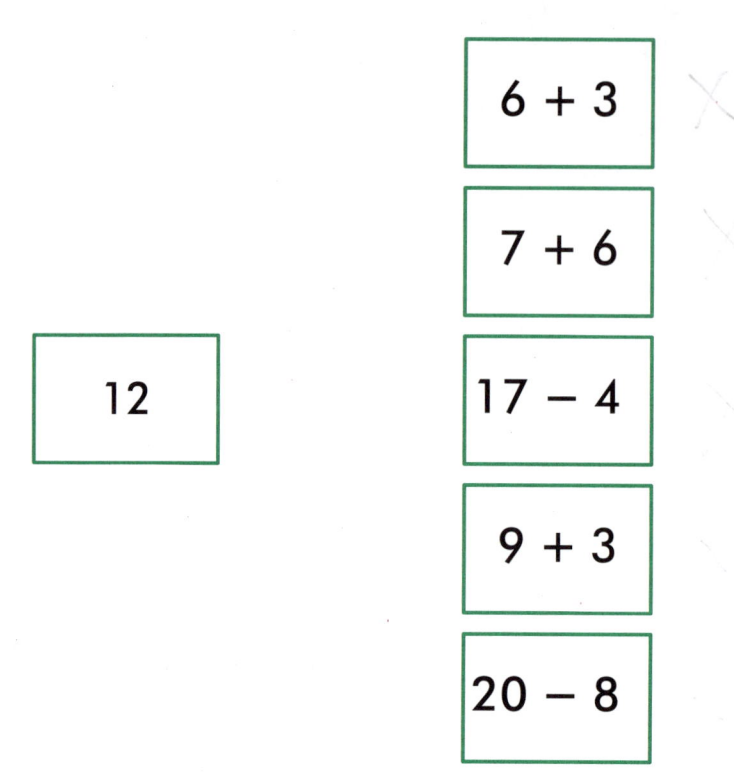

6 + 3

7 + 6

12   17 − 4

9 + 3

20 − 8

16 Write in the missing numbers.

5   15   ☐   35   ☐   55

17 Sumhil has a pencil case.
In it are **3** blue pencils, **5** red pencils and **2** green pencils.
How many pencils altogether?

☐ pencils

18 Draw a ring around the **cube**.

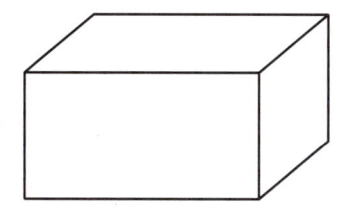

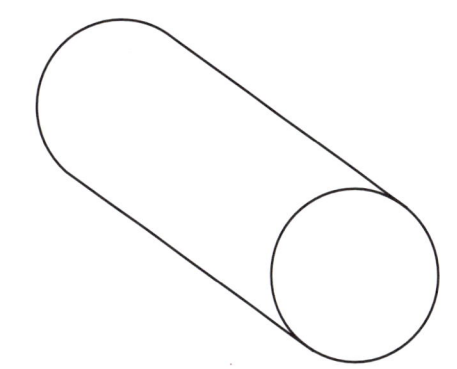

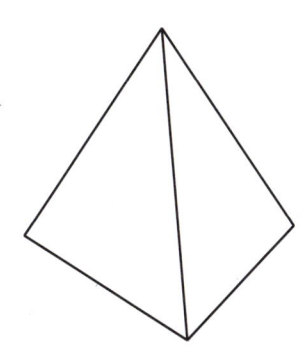

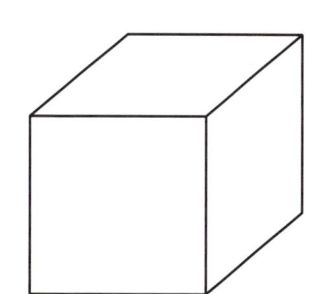

19 Look at these numbers.

8   6   3   7   4

Use **three** numbers to make a sum adding to **18**.

☐ + ☐ + ☐ = 18

20 Find the answer

76 − 54 = ☐

21 Put a number in the box to make this sum correct.

$$26 + 3 = 50 - \boxed{}$$

22 Finish this number pattern.

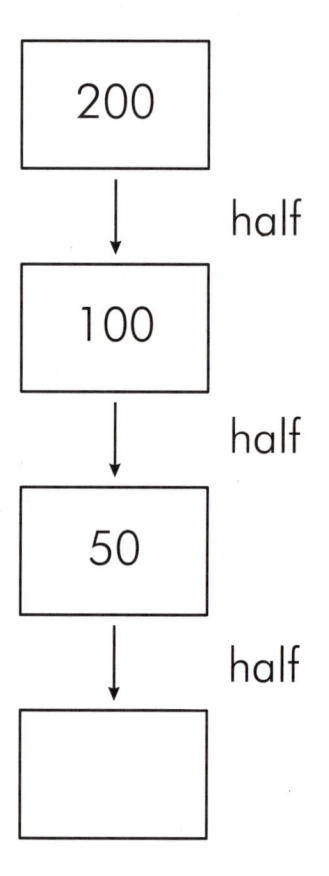

200 → half → 100 → half → 50 → half → ☐

23 Mr Speed went to a football match.

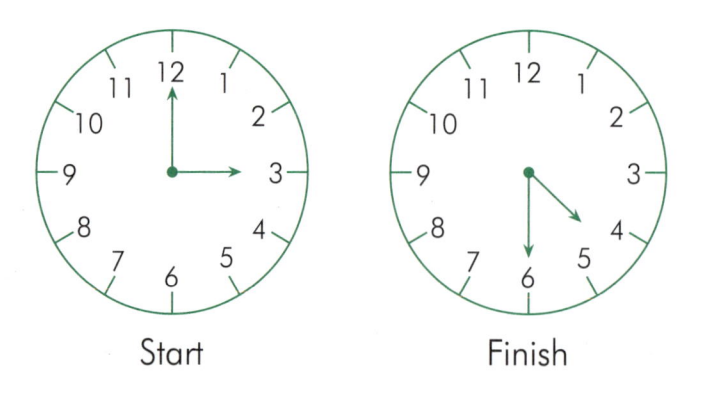

Start / Finish

How many **minutes** was he there? ☐

24

Mario's Ices			
Tub	65p	Choc Ice	40p
Lolly	55p	Cornet	45p

(a) Which two things can you buy for exactly £1?

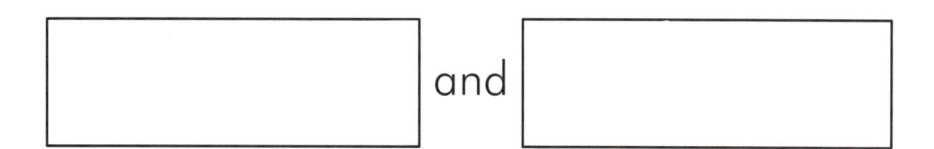

☐ and ☐

(b) How much do a **choc ice** and a **tub** cost together?

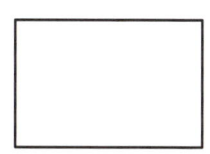

☐

25 Fill in the missing numbers in the correct order.

221   201   121

101 ☐ 200 ☐ 210 ☐ 312

26 Shastha has **£1.59** in her purse. She has **5** coins.
Put a circle around all the coins she has.

27 A fraction of each shape is shaded.
Tick (✓) the shapes which show $\frac{1}{2}$.

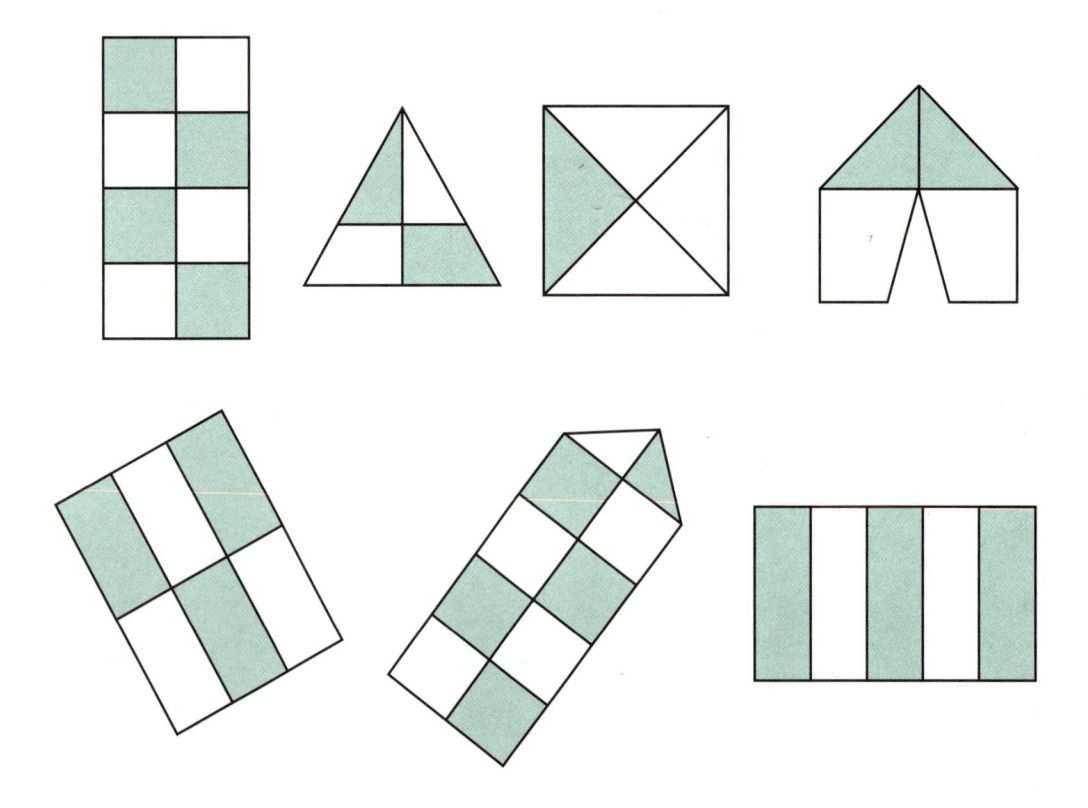

28 Jody sorted these numbers. **Two** numbers are in the wrong place.

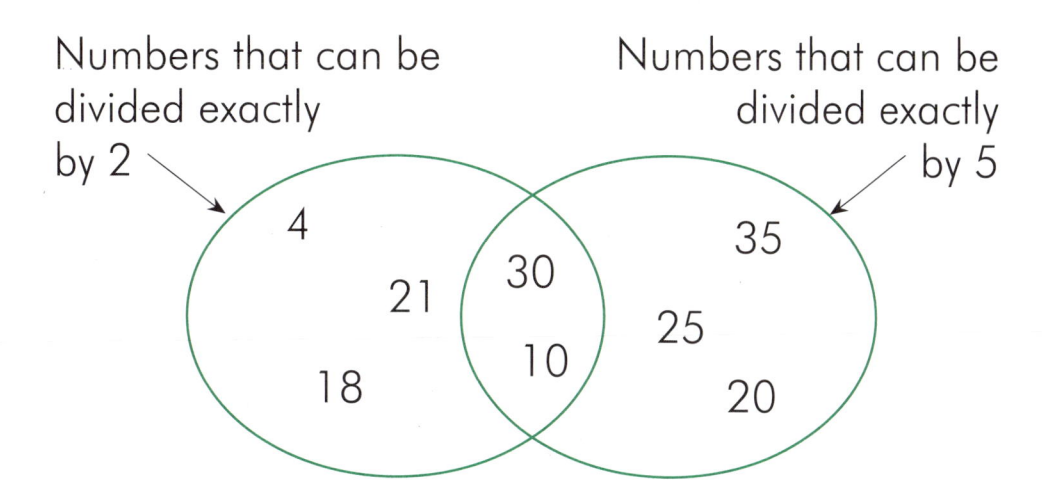

Numbers that can be divided exactly by 2

Numbers that can be divided exactly by 5

4, 21, 30, 35, 25, 10, 18, 20

Cross out the numbers in the wrong place.

29 Put a number in the box to make this correct.

☐ × 7 = 70

30 How heavy is the box?

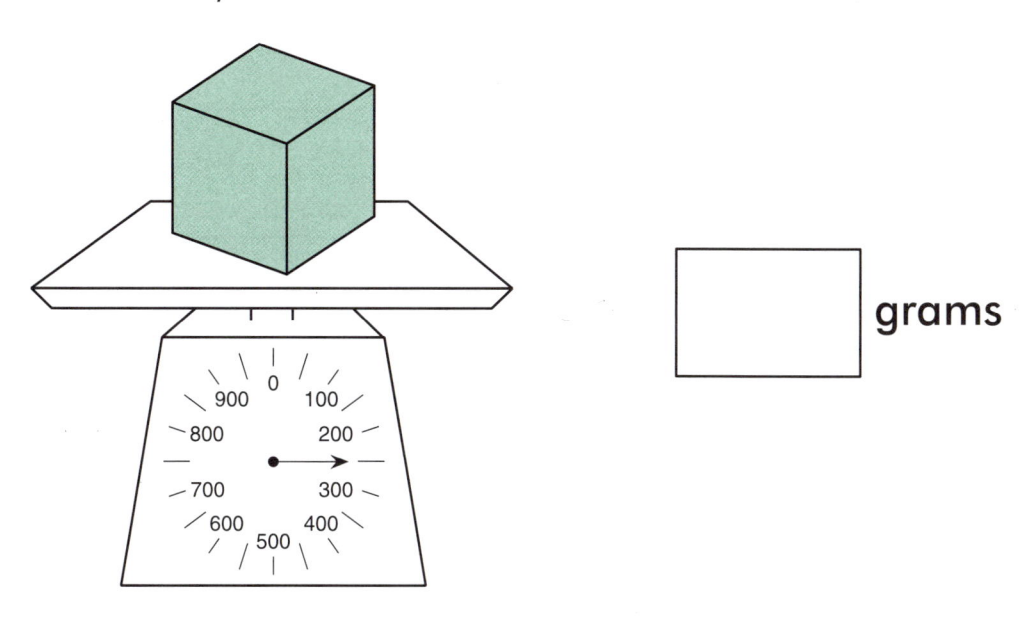

☐ grams

31 Write the missing number.

700 subtract 1 is ☐

32 This table shows what 6 children had for breakfast.

	Coffee	Tea	Bacon and egg	Cereal	Toast
Amelia	✓		✓		
Fred		✓			✓
Zahir				✓	✓
Sally		✓			✓
James		✓	✓		✓
Ella	✓			✓	

(a) What did Sally have? ☐

(b) Who ate cereal and toast? ☐

(c) How many children had toast? ☐

MATHEMATICS
Test C

1 Write the number **thirty five** in figures.

2 Put a tick (✓) in the **rectangle**.

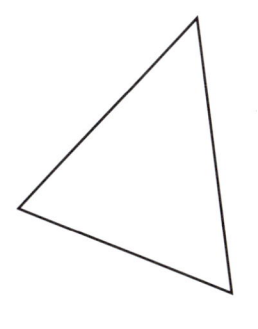

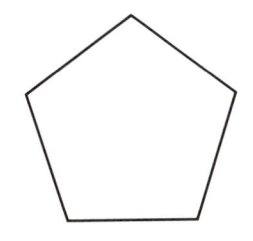

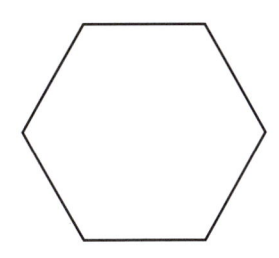

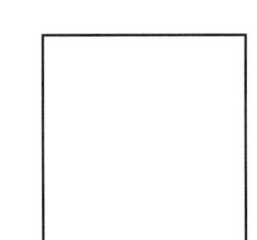

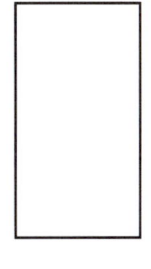

3 Add **nine** and **six**.

4 What is the next number?

3   5   7   9

5 How much money is in the purse?

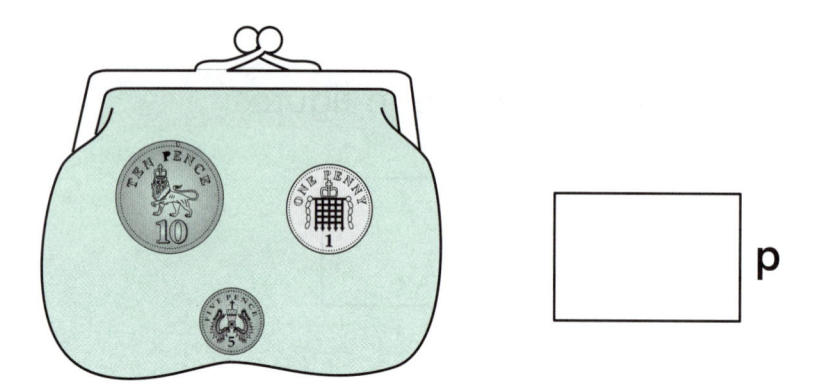

☐ p

6 Which number is the arrow pointing to?
Write it in the box.

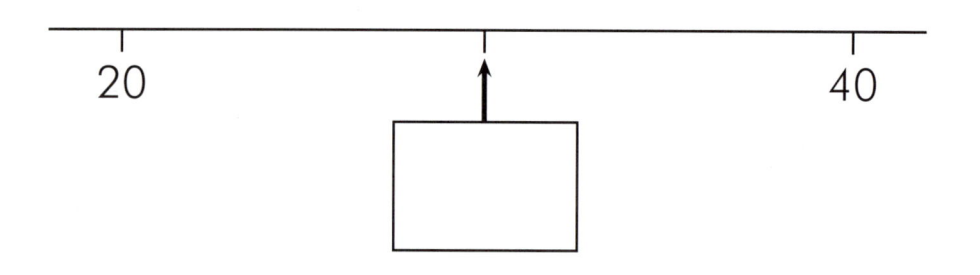

20 ————↑———— 40

☐

7 Write the answer to the sum.

24 − 9 = ☐

8 Join dots to draw **two** squares. Make each square a different size.

9 How heavy are the apples?

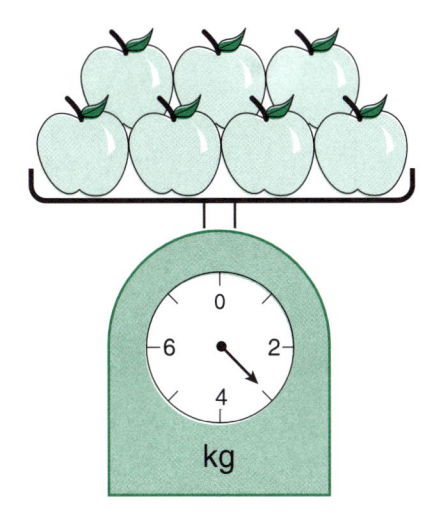

☐ kg

10 Fill in the missing number.

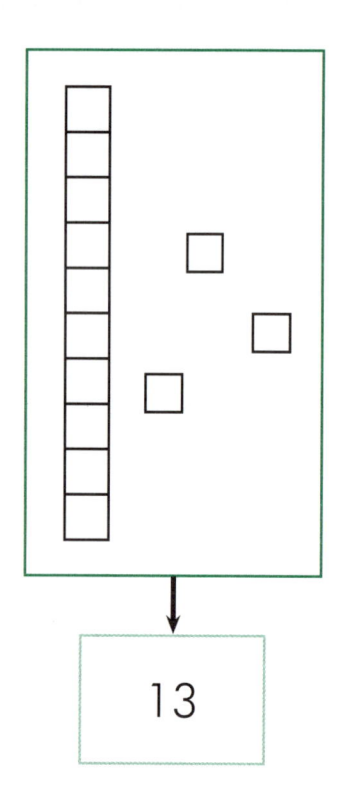

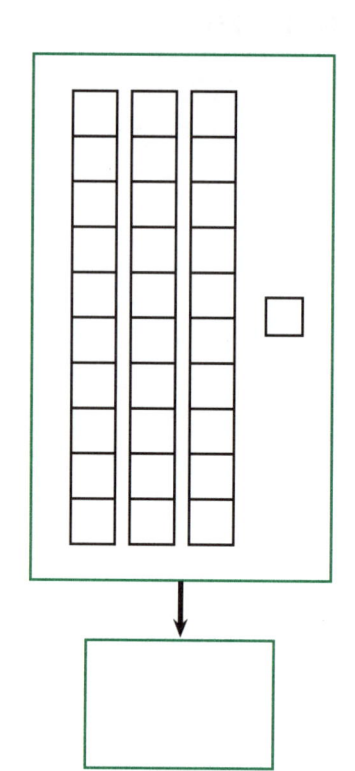

13

11 Look at these numbers

32   19   51   68

Which number is **less than** 30?

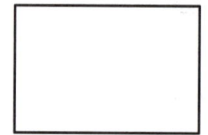

12 Which number from question 11 is **between** 40 and 60?

13 Join two dots which are **10 centimetres** apart. (You may use a ruler.)

14 This graph shows the colour of some children's eyes.

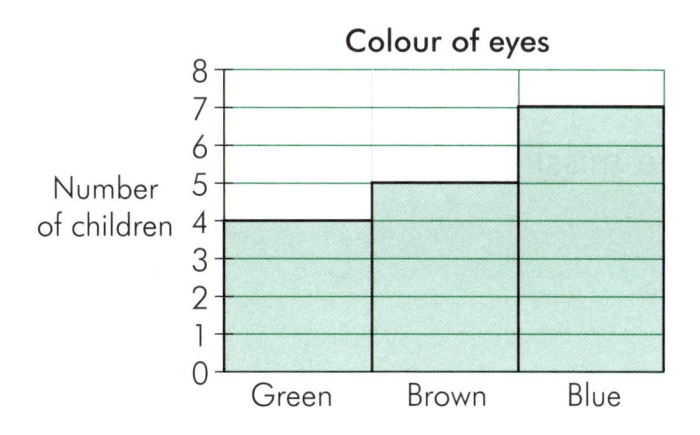

Colour of eyes

Number of children

(a) How many children have **brown** eyes?

(b) How many **more** children have blue eyes than green eyes?

15 Colour $\frac{1}{2}$ of this shape.

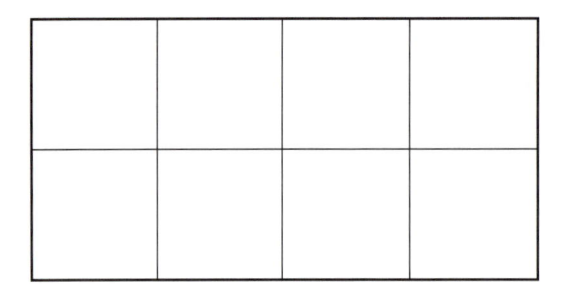

16 Write three **even** numbers which are **more** than 10 and **less** than 30.

17 Draw **all** the missing lines.

Three tens — 7

Half of 8 — 30

10 minus 3 — 15

7 add 8 — 4

18 Write the correct number in the box.

$$48 - \boxed{} = 15$$

19 This table shows the number of children at three schools.

School	Number
Woodlands	206
Dunn Road	198
Littlemore	255

Tick (✓) the school with the **most** children.

20 Look at these shapes.

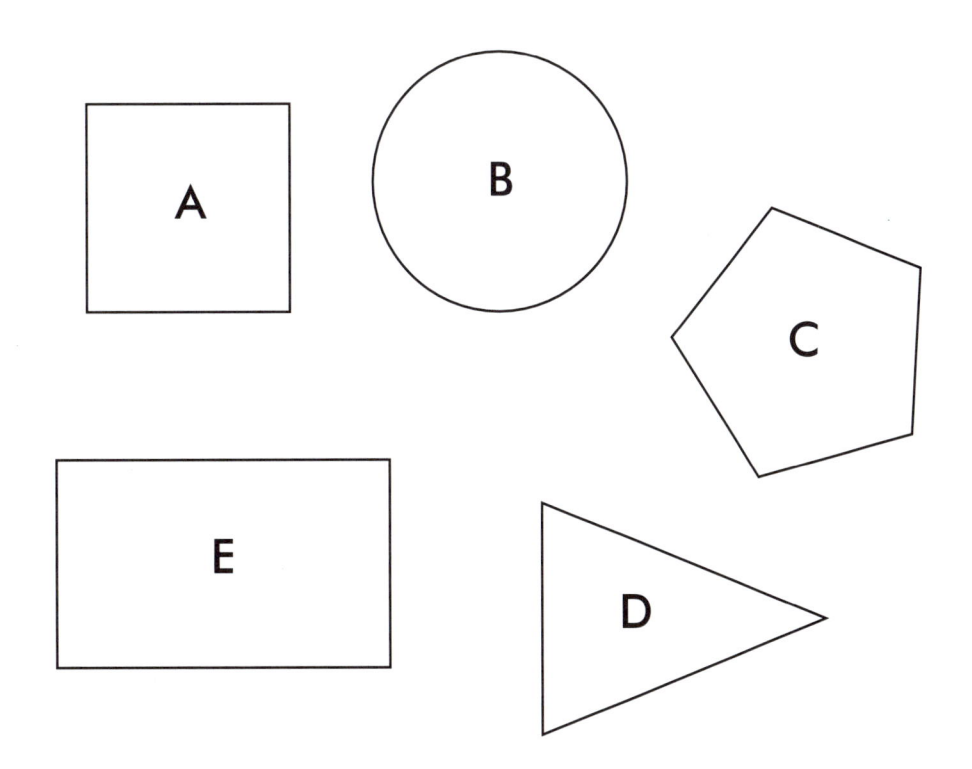

Which shapes have **right angles**?

☐ and ☐

21 Write any numbers you like in the squares so that all six numbers are in order.

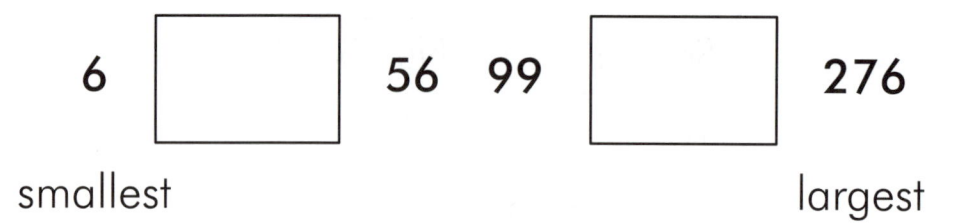

6 ☐ 56 99 ☐ 276

smallest   largest

22 Draw the reflection of the shape in the mirror line.

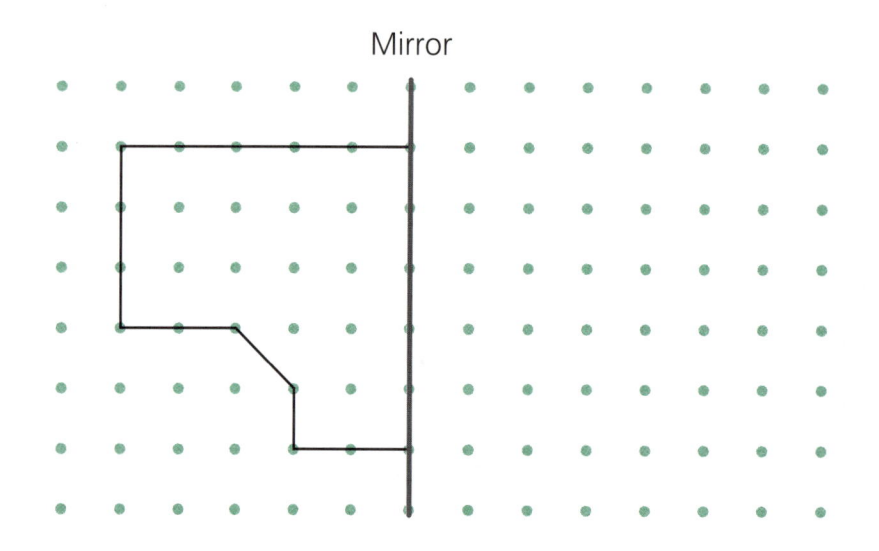

Mirror

23 Write signs to make these sums correct. (Use + or −)

26 ☐ 19 = 7

23 ☐ 9 = 32

24 Complete this sequence.

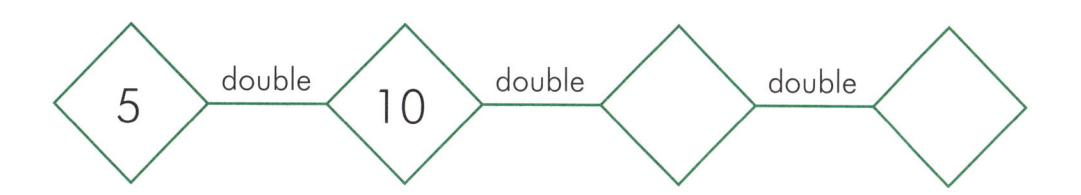

5 —double— 10 —double— ☐ —double— ☐

25 Circle all numbers that can be divided **exactly** by 10.

20   160   283

81   266   320

26 This jar has sweets.
Mary and John guessed how many sweets there were.

Mary said **44**.
John said **38**.

They counted the sweets.
There were 40. Tick (✓) who had the **nearest** guess.

27 An ice cream costs **25p**.
How much will **5** cost?

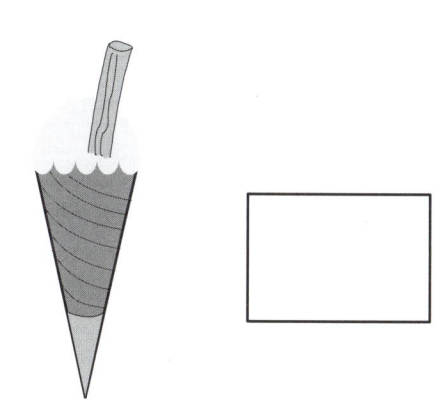

28 How many ice creams costing 25p can you buy for £1.00?

29 Write a number in the box to make this sum correct.

$$56 + \boxed{} = 100$$

30 Write a number in the box to make this sum correct.

$$40 \div 10 = \boxed{} \times 2$$

31 This chart shows how some children get to school.

Travelling to school

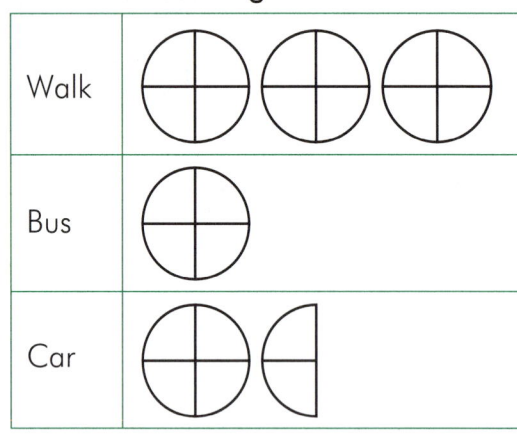

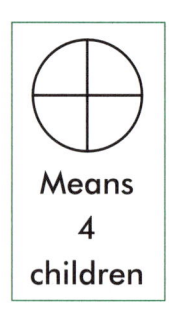

Walk	⊕ ⊕ ⊕
Bus	⊕
Car	⊕ ◐

Means 4 children

(a) How many children walk to school?

(b) How many children come by car?

☐

(c) How many **more** children walk to school than travel by bus?

☐

32 Write numbers in the boxes to make this correct.

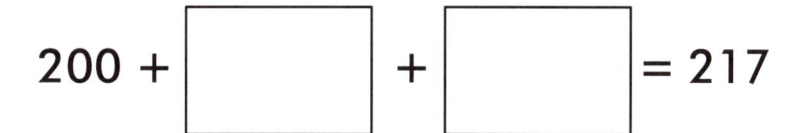

200 + ☐ + ☐ = 217

PART 2

Answers

Marking the tests

- When marking your child's test, complete the **marking grid** on page 62.
- Find the total number of marks that your child has achieved in this test.
- Refer to the **table** at the bottom of the marking grid to find the Level achieved.
- Remember that the Levels given are intended only as an indication of how your child has performed in this test. With further practice and experience your child's performance can be improved.
- At Key Stage 1, Level 2 covers a wide spread of ability. It is customary to divide this Level into three parts:

Level 2C   Your child is at the threshold of Level 2
Level 2B   Your child is in the middle of Level 2
Level 2A   Your child is towards the top of Level 2

Answers to Test A

1 16 is the next number after 14

> Your child should recognise the pattern, either that it involves a series of *even* numbers in rising order or that two is added each time, from one number to the next.

2 26

> Your child needs to be able to place digits (whole numbers) in the correct order when writing down numbers. Here the first number is for the tens (2 of them) and the second number for the units (6 of them).

3 17p

> The question tests your child's ability to add a single digit number (7) to a double digit number (10).

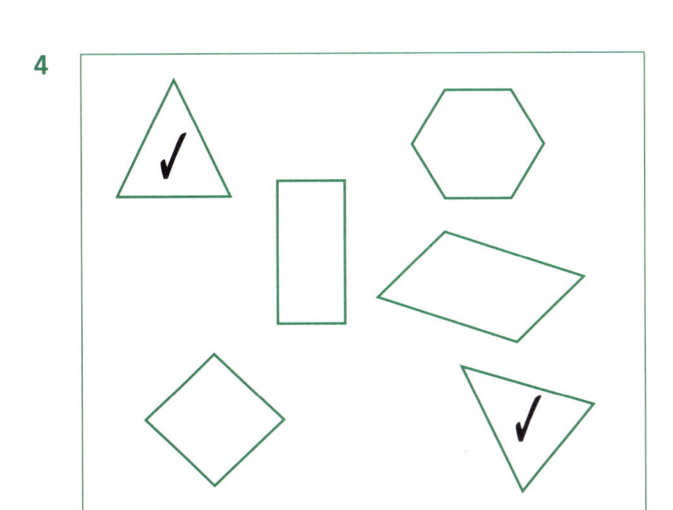

4

> Your child needs to understand and use the vocabulary associated with shapes. Looking at objects around the home and identifying their shape and name will help here. Triangles are shapes with three straight sides.

5 10 − 2 has 8 as the answer

> This question involves simple addition and subtraction. The more children practice this, the more confident and accurate they will become. Notice that the word 'sum' as used here can mean either add or subtract (or multiply or divide in other situations).

6 31, 32, 33

> Recognising that the pattern *increases by 1* is quite straightforward. If your child is confident with this, practice using larger numbers and rather more difficult patterns.

7 The even numbers are 16, 18, 28 and 50

> Your child does need to understand the idea of an *even* number, i.e. numbers that divide exactly by two. You might point this out using houses down one side of a road, etc.

8 4 apples should have been ringed or circled

> This idea of two equal parts is important, and links in with the two times table again. Get your child to recognise that dividing a number in half is the *opposite* to multiplying the answer by two. So half of 8 apples is 4 apples and 2 × 4 apples = 8 apples.

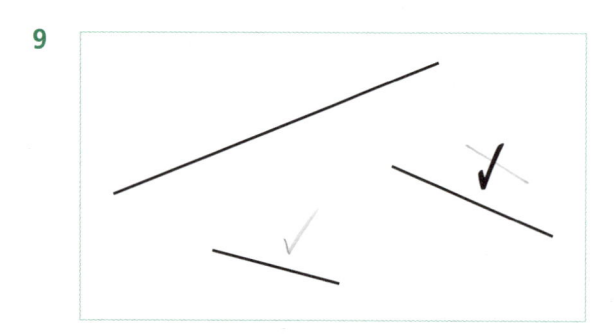

9

> The question requires your child to use a ruler accurately and to understand and use the unit of length we call centimetres. You could ask your child to measure the other lines in centimetres, for practice.

10 10 o'clock

> Telling the time is an important skill. Children need to understand the importance of the position of the hour hand (the short hand) and the minute hand (the long hand). Make sure your child is familiar with the time when the minute hand is on the hour, on the half hour and at the quarters.

11

Right angles can be easily identified as the corners of windows and doors. They need to be identified in shapes as being quite special and different from other angles. Rectangles and squares will have right angles.

12 58p

If your child regularly handles amounts of money and is encouraged to say how much they have, then this type of problem will seem quite straightforward.

13 There are several correct answers, such as:
$10 + 1$ or $9 + 2$ or $8 + 3$ or $7 + 4$ or $6 + 5$
or any of these the other way round

Some children find this type of problem difficult as they are more used to finding the *answer* to a sum! You could practice this kind of question with your child, drawing two (or even three) shapes and choosing different numbers for the answer.

14 (a) Two faces should be drawn in the green column
(b) $5 - 3 = 2$

Children enjoy pictograms, and using them helps to develop confidence in extracting and interpreting information, skills that are required for work in data handling.
(This pictogram has one face for one child. You can develop this skill by asking what the answers would have been if the one face represented *two* children.)

15 Any of 34, 37, 43 or 47

Using the term 'less than' (and also greater or more than) can cause some children confusion. Ask your child to tell you numbers in response to statements like 'a number less than 20' or 'a number bigger than 40'.

16

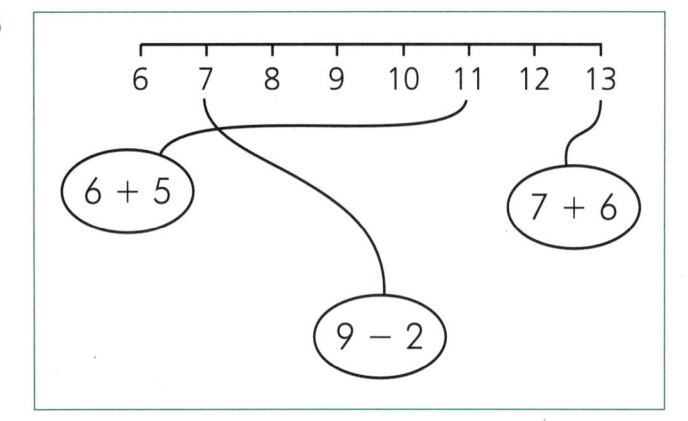

```
    6  7  8  9  10 11 12 13
       |_____|
       |     _____|
  ( 6 + 5 )       ( 7 + 6 )
              |
          ( 9 − 2 )
```

> Again 'sum' can mean add or subtract here. This type of question checks on the basic number bonds that your child should be making. Again, practising these bonds will help to secure them into their memory.

17 21 dots.

> It is important that your child understands mathematical words that mean 'add', such as 'sum of', 'total', 'how many altogether'.

18 52, 85, 117, 123, 198, 232

> This question is about *ordering* numbers. It is important your child recognises the need to pick out the *two digit* numbers first, as these are smaller than the *three digit* numbers. Then look for the one with the smallest first digit to give the smallest overall number (52). The next step is to look at the three digit numbers and to find those with the smallest first digit (1) and then use the second digit to put these in order. Eventually, of course, we learn to do this almost instinctively, but we are actually going through this type of procedure.

19 300 − 1 = 299
    200 − 1 = 199

> Your child should recognise the pattern of subtracting one from a number that is itself falling by 100 each time. If this does cause problems, then practice using smaller numbers to help develop their confidence in identifying this type of problem.

20 5 o'clock

> Counting forwards and backwards in time is something that can be practised using clocks and watches in the home.

21 35

> This problem needs recognising as the type that is best done by putting the numbers in a column, biggest on top and subtracting. Notice how we change a ten to units in this subtraction.
>
> $\begin{array}{r} {}^4\cancel{5}{}^1 2 \\ -\ 1\ 7 \\ \hline 3\ 5 \end{array}$ Because we cannot subtract 7 from 2, we need to take a ten away from the 5 tens (replace 5 with a 4) and add this ten to the two units to make twelve units. Now we can do the subtraction.
>
> This is how your child will be shown to do subtraction at school. Make sure you do follow what is happening so that you can help your child.

22 15p

> Encourage the use of adding on to solve this problem. 'I need another 10p to make it 60p, then I need another 5p to make the 65p. So I need 10p + 5p altogether, which is 15p.' Of course subtracting 50p from 65p, will give the correct answer, but children often find the 'adding on' method easier.

23

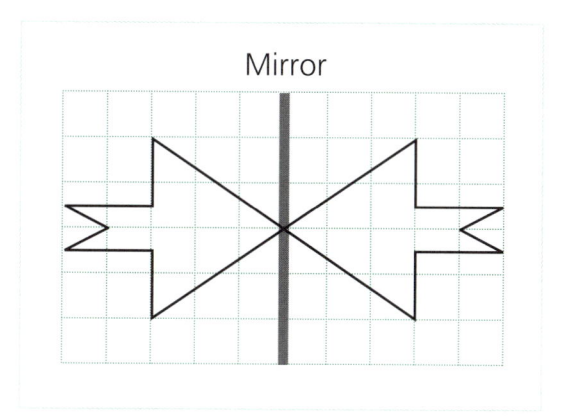

Mirror

> Use a mirror to give your child experience of reflective symmetry. Talk to them about what is happening. (The mirror will complete the shape exactly.)

24

17	139
12	152

5
126

> This is a *Carroll Diagram*, and is used to help children sort out information. Your child needs encouraging to think about the different *types* of numbers on each axis.

25 (a) Wednesday   (b) Monday   (c) 5 hours

> This question requires your child to interpret and extract information from a vertical bar chart. Check that your child understands the scale on the vertical axis (hours of sunshine). You can practice by asking extra questions about the chart.

26 112

This problem can be seen as one in which the tens add up to 100, the units add up to 12, so put these together and the whole sum adds up to 100 + 12 which is 112

27

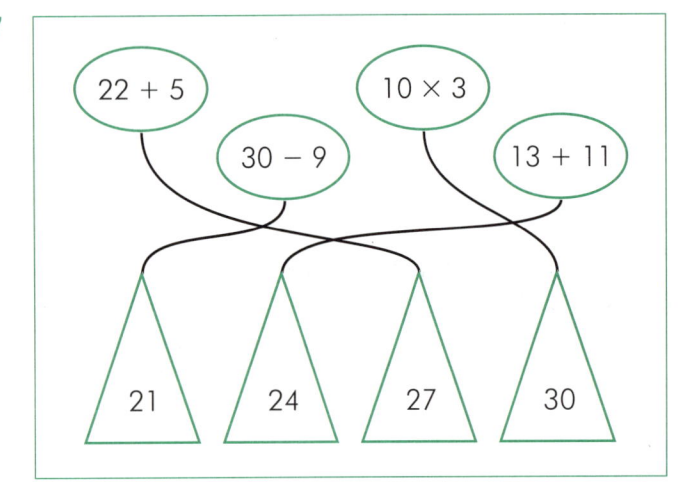

- 22 + 5 → 27
- 30 − 9 → 21
- 10 × 3 → 30
- 13 + 11 → 24

Remember a 'sum' can be add, subtract, multiply or divide. This problem is best tackled by doing the simple ones first and seeing what is left. The 10 × 3 may well be the first one to do, then maybe 22 + 5, then 13 + 11, leaving the most difficult 30 − 9 as the only one left. Of course your child may well have done these in quite a different order if a particular type of sum presents no problem to them.

28 62

Your child should be discouraged from just trying different numbers, but should use the 'adding on' method again. Add on 2 to get to 140, then add on 60 to get up to 200. This gives us 2 + 60 = 62 needed.

29 590

Your child needs to see that each small line in between the numbers shown is going up in tens. Subtraction (610 − 560 = 50) and division (50 ÷ 5 spaces = 10) may help here. We then go up 3 small lines from 560 to give 590.

30

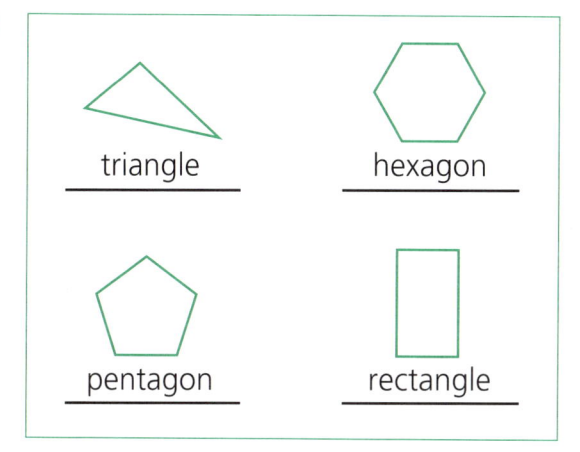

triangle	hexagon
pentagon	rectangle

> Children do get confused with the names of these shapes. The most difficult being the pentagon (5 sides) and the hexagon (6 sides). One helpful hint, is to remember that 'hex' is similar to six and so hexagon has 6 sides.

31 6 boys

> In problems like this, children are often unsure as to the mathematical operation they are supposed to be using. Point out that to have a total number of 18 children would suggest that the number of boys is less than 18. The answer can be found either by 'add on' 6 boys to the 12 girls *or* by subtract 12 girls from 18 children to give 6 boys.

32 25, 30, 50 and 100 should be ringed

> Your child should be encouraged to recognise that only numbers that end in a 5 or 0 are exactly divisible by 5

Answers to Test B

1 58

> Children need to appreciate the importance of place value – that is, of writing digits (whole numbers) in the correct order. Here the tens digit (5) comes before the units digit (8).

2

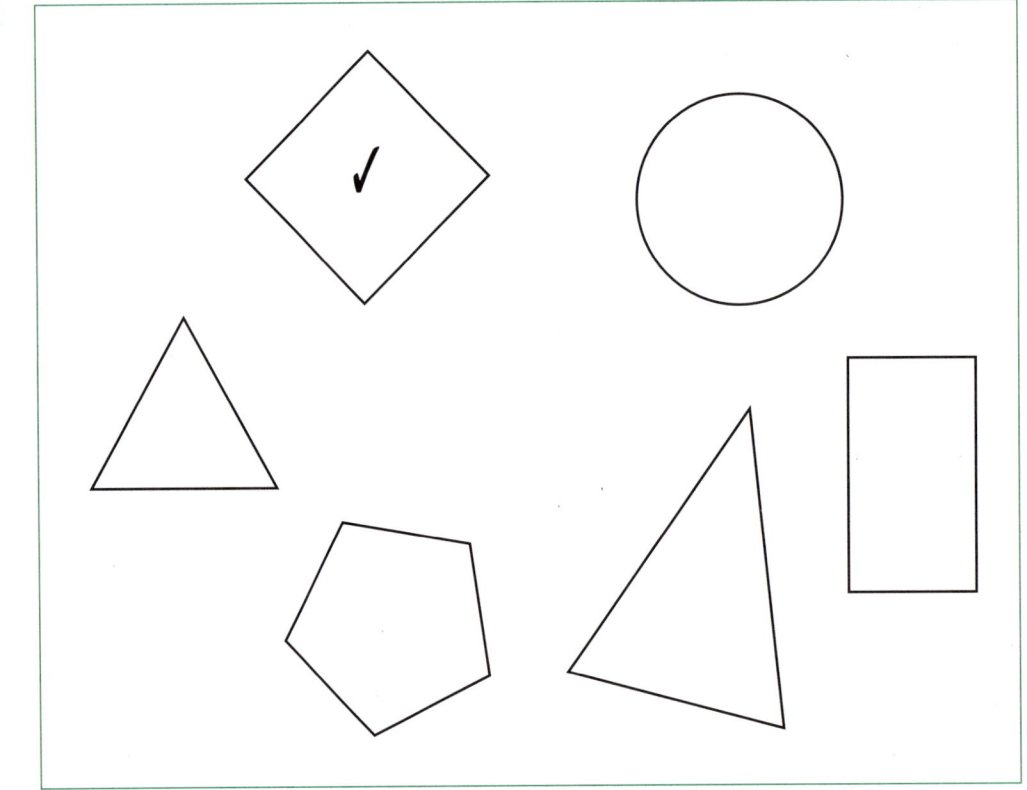

(Tick on the diamond/square shape)

> Encourage your child to recognise different 2-D shapes. They should be able to tell you that a square has four equal sides. Use objects around the home and use correct mathematical vocabulary (e.g. rectangle and not oblong, circle and not round). Many children will insist this square is a diamond; encourage them to turn the book round to see it is square.

3 11

> This is a simple number bond that your child may know, or can solve by simply counting on three starting from eight. Remember that words such as 'total', 'sum of', 'how many altogether', suggest *add*.

4 38p

Add up the coins involving tens first to get 30p (20p + 10p) then add the pence to get 8p, now put both of these together to make 38p

5 3 is the smallest number

A confusion is sometimes to think that 12 is smaller than 3 because the digits (1 and 2) are smaller. So encourage your child to recognise that a *two* digit number always has tens, so is bigger than a *single* digit number.

6 5

A common starting point is the 4 and then count on 5 to reach the 9. Eventually your child will see that they could just subtract 4 from 9 to give 5

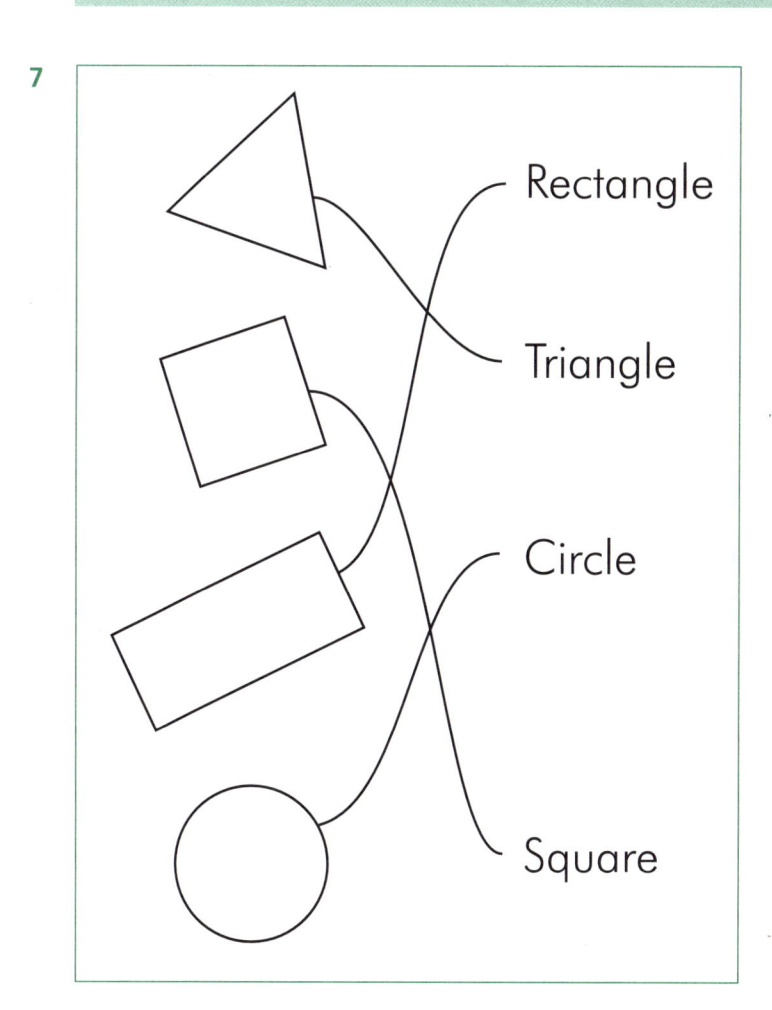

7

Triangle — triangle shape
Square — square shape
Rectangle — rectangle shape
Circle — circle shape

It is important that your child can recognise the basic shapes and give them the correct name. The biggest confusion is perhaps between square and rectangle; do check that your child has got them the right way round! Practice naming shapes around the home.

ANSWERS TEST B

8 Either 5 flowers should be coloured or each of the 10 flowers has a half of it coloured.

> With either answer your child should be showing some recognition of what a half is, namely two equal parts. A half of ten could have been found by 10 ÷ 2 = 5

9

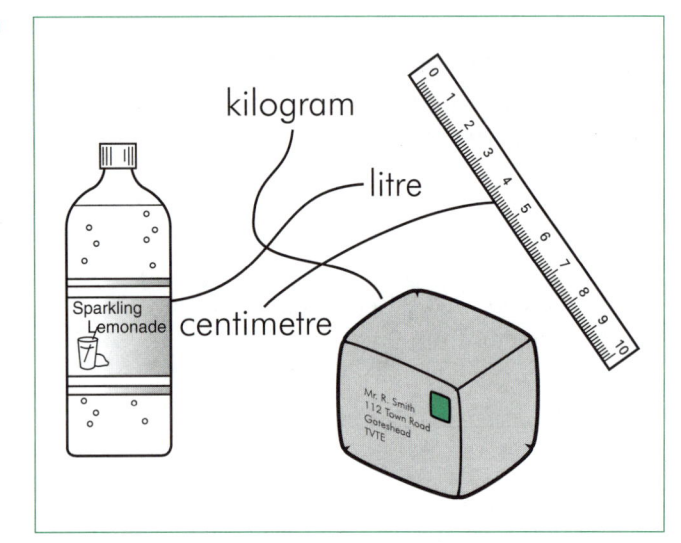

- bottle of Sparkling Lemonade — litre
- ruler — centimetre
- parcel — kilogram

> Your child should be encouraged to be familiar with the *type of unit* used to measure length, weight and capacity. Although you may use *imperial* units, be aware that the children should be familiar with the *metric* units as well as the imperial units. Your child should link litre (capacity) with lemonade and centimetre (length) with measuring objects such as a ruler.

10

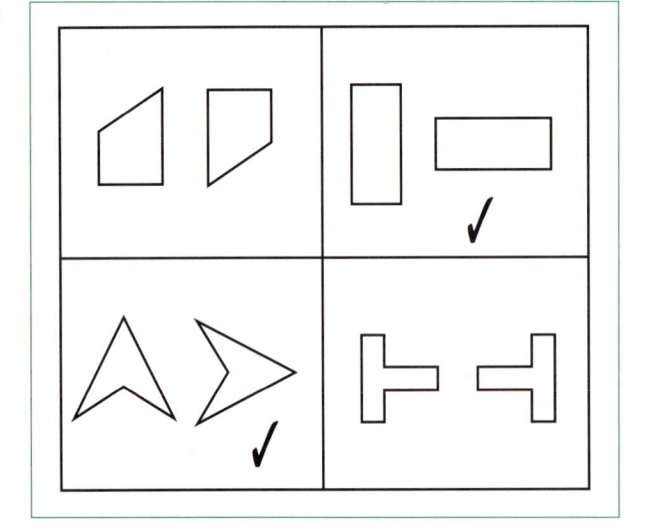

Top-right shape (rectangle) ✓
Bottom-left shape (arrow) ✓

> Tracing paper can be a great help here; trace the shape then turn it through a right angle and see if it looks correct. Do not worry about clockwise and anticlockwise at this stage unless your child mentions it.

52

11 Any *three* numbers from the list: 1, 3, 5, 7, 9, 11, 13, 15, 17 or 19

> The word *odd* does need to be understood by your child. It is a number that will not share equally into two.

12 5 cakes

> Your child may have worked their way to the answer by seeing that two cakes would be 20p then three cakes would be 30p. They may then have made the leap to five cakes being 50p. Alternatively $50 \div 10 = 5$ or $10 \times 5 = 50$. Knowing their 5 times or ten times table could help here.

13 5, 16, 29, 35, 61, 92

> Your child should recognise that 5, as the *single digit*, is the smallest number. Then encourage them to look at the tens in the *two digit* numbers, i.e. at the first of the two digits. They should then have been able to write the numbers from smallest to largest.

14 (a) Amil has 2 pets
(b) Harry

> This question is testing if your child can interpret tables and diagrams. Check they can read the information on this type of chart.

15 Lines should be drawn to the $9 + 3$ and $20 - 8$ boxes

> Number bonds are an important basis of arithmetical knowledge. To be able to recognise number bonds up to twelve will be very useful to your child.

16 25 and 45

> This question requires your child to identify the pattern of the numbers before finding the missing numbers. The 5's should give them the hint that each number is 10 more than the one before.

17 10 pencils

> This question is about recognising the need to *add up* the given numbers. There are quite a few different ways to be asked to add up: words such as 'sum of', 'total' and 'how many altogether?'

18

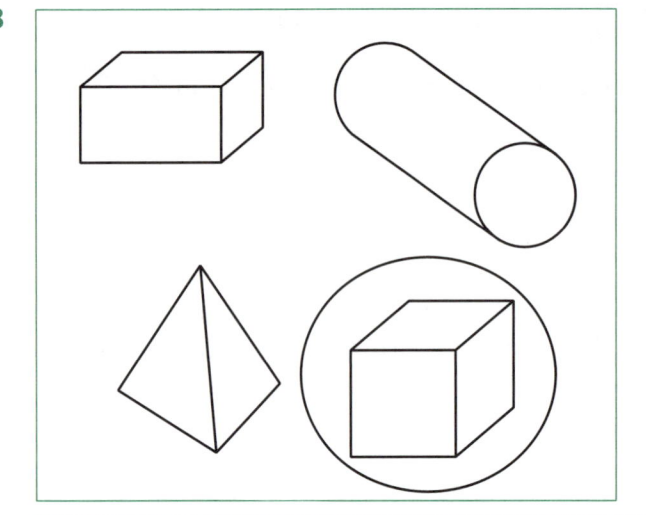

Some children find this type of 3D representation difficult. It is well worth getting your child to practice drawing a 3D cube and cuboid to help reinforce what they look like on paper.

19 4 + 6 + 8 = 18 *or* 3 + 7 + 8 = 18
(the numbers can be in any order)

It is helpful to look for links (or bonds) to 18. For example your child should know that 10 + 8 = 18, and so might look for a *combination* to give 10 as well as the 8 already there. This would lead to either answer above.

20 22

Encourage your child to set out the problem vertically and to do the subtraction as shown.

```
  7 6
- 5 4
  ───
  2 2
```

Or your child might have tried the *building up* method of adding 2 to get 56, then a further 20 to get 76, giving 2 + 20 = 22 as the answer.

21 21

Children will get confused when the sum does not appear as they are used to seeing it. Here they should be encouraged to make it look more friendly by moving and sorting first. For example they might make the question into 50 − ? = 29. This may help them to see what has to be added to 29 to get back to 50, namely a one to get to thirty, then a further twenty, to give 21 altogether.

22 25 is a half of 50

It is good practice both halving and doubling different numbers. It is this type of practice that will help your child remember that 25 can be doubled to give 50. A useful check on a halving problem is to double the answer and get the value to be halved.

23 90 minutes

Your child needs to know that there are 60 minutes in the hour, and thirty in half an hour. Put these together to make 90 minutes. Practice time questions using clocks and watches in the home.

24 (a) Lolly and Cornet (b) £1.05 *or* 105p

Your child needs to know that £1 is the same as 100p, then to spot the numbers that will add up to 100. For part (b) your child should be encouraged to write the units down correctly, either in pence or in pounds.

25 121, 201, 221

It is important to be able to recognise the relative size of the numbers, to know that the *first digit* in each of these three digit numbers is the hundreds, and the *middle digit* is the tens, with the *last digit* being the units.

26 The £1, 50p, 5p, and both 2p coins should be circled

It is worth using the *build up* method here. To make £1 from the pound coin, then 50p from the fifty pence coin, now they just have to make up 9p from the five pence and 2 two pence coins.

27

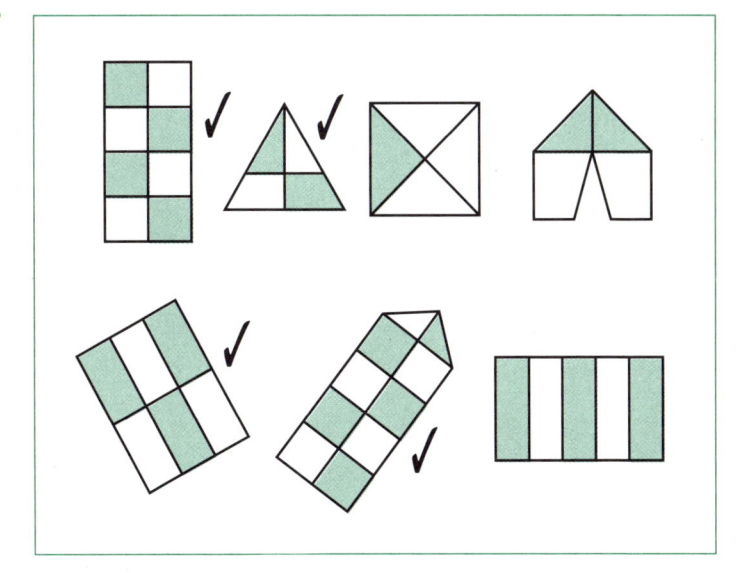

It is this idea of two equal parts that is important to recognise for a half. They may count the number of equal pieces just to make sure.

28 The 20 and the 21 should be crossed out

> This is not an easy chart to understand. It is the *overlap* that may need explaining – that these numbers are in *both* regions. The 21 was probably spotted but the 20 would be the most difficult as it does divide exactly by 5, however it can also be divided exactly by 2 and so should be in the *overlap* region.

29 10

> It is vital to learn the ten times table, it is a basis on which so much is built.

30 250 grams

> There is a need to recognise that halfway between 200 and 300 is 250, and that we are dealing with grams as a unit of weight.

31 699

> Subtracting one from a large number can be tricky for children. If your child does find this difficult, then encourage thinking about smaller numbers first; for example one from 20, then one from 100 and build up to one from 700.

32 (a) Sally had tea and toast
(b) Zahir had cereal and toast
(c) 4 children had toast.

> Interpreting tables is an important part of Data Handling. Children may be confused by the number of columns and rows. They can be encouraged to use a ruler to help them follow a line of information. Sometimes this type of chart is drawn with crosses in the places where there is no tick.

Answers to Test C

1 35

> Children need to be able to place the digits of the number in the correct order. Here the first digit (3) represents tens and the second digit (5) represents units.

2

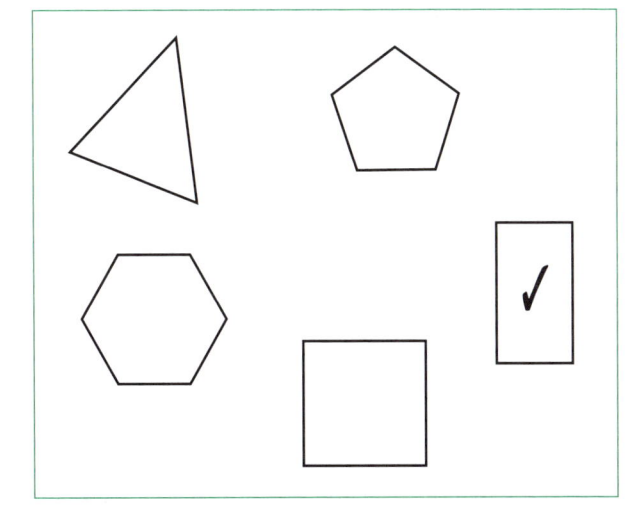

> It is important that children recognise 2D shapes and use the correct vocabulary (e.g. rectangle not oblong). Check that your child understands the difference between a square (4 equal sides) and a rectangle (opposite sides are equal).

3 15

> Children need plenty of practice with number bonds to 20. Help your child by showing them how to count on from the starting number (in this case count 6 on from nine) using their fingers or a number line.

4 11 is the next number after 9

> Your child should recognise the pattern of odd numbers or understand that the sequence involves numbers increasing by 2 each time.

5 16p

> Encourage your child to look for tens. Then look for coins with the value of units (5p, 2p or 1p) and add them to the total of the tens.

6 30

Your child needs to recognise that the divisions are in tens. Another strategy is to show your child that the missing number is halfway between 20 and 40 i.e. 30.

7 15

The question can be tackled by counting on from 9 to 24. Another method is to recognise that 9 is one away from 10. So 24 subtract 10 is 14, then add the 1.

8 (a) One mark for drawing shapes which have *equal* sides
(b) One mark for drawing squares of *different* sizes

It is important that your child uses the dots when drawing shapes. Some children find this difficult and need plenty of practice.

9 3 kg

There is a need to recognise that the arrow is pointing towards 3 (halfway between 2 and 4) and that the units of measurement are kilograms.

10 31

Your child needs to understand the importance of place value – writing the tens digit (3) before the units digit (1).

11 19

Your child may be confused by the term 'less than'. Ask your child to tell you numbers which answer statements like 'a number less than 20'. This can be extended to include the term 'greater than', before progressing to 'numbers *between*' given numbers (question 12).

12 51

Count with your child from 40 to 60 and explain that 41 to 59 are the numbers *between*. If your child finds this difficult start with a smaller difference i.e. 40 and 50.

13

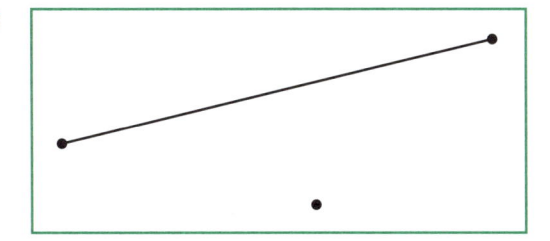

The question requires your child to measure accurately with a ruler, and understand the unit of measurement for length.

14 (a) 5
(b) 3 (7 subtract 4)

This question requires your child to understand and extract information from a bar chart. It is important that your child understands the scale on the vertical axis.
You can practice reading bar charts by asking extra questions about the chart.

15 Four squares should be shaded

It is important that your child understands the idea of two equal parts and checks that their answer is correct by counting.

16 Any three numbers from: 12, 14, 16, 18, 20, 22, 24, 26, 28

Your child should remember that even numbers can be divided exactly by 2 and end in the digits 0, 2, 4, 6 or 8.

17 Lines should be drawn from
Three tens   to   30
Half of 8   to   4
7 add 8   to   15

Show your child how to look at the sums and identify the operations needing to be used. Encourage them to start by finding the answer to the sum with which they are most confident.

18 33

Children may become confused when the sum does not appear as they are used to seeing it. If, as in this case, the second number in a subtraction sum is missing, show your child how to change the sum around:
48 − 15 = which will give the answer 33.

ANSWERS TEST C

19 Littlemore has the most children (255)

> This requires understanding of hundreds, tens and units. Encourage your child to sort numbers in order of size by giving them extra practice.

20 A and E

> Your child needs to understand the properties of 2D shapes. Once they are confident about naming shapes, encourage them to look at the number of sides and angles.

21 There are many possible correct answers, the first number being between 6 and 56, the second between 99 and 276.

> Your child may find this difficult if they are looking for a number pattern. In fact, numbers in order do not need to have a pattern linking them all.

22

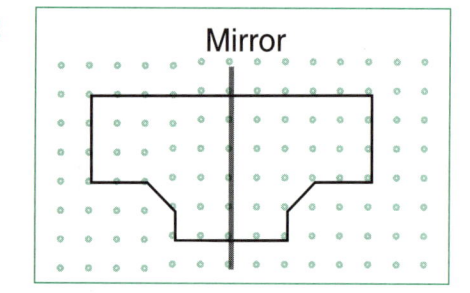

> Use a mirror to help your child see reflective symmetry. (The mirror will complete the shape exactly.)

23 $26 - 19 = 7$
$23 + 9 = 32$

> In questions like this encourage your child to look at all the information, especially the answer. If the answer (e.g. 32) is larger than the numbers (23 and 9) then try addition. If the answer is smaller than the numbers try substraction.

24 20, 40

> It is good to practise both halving and doubling numbers.
> A useful check on a doubling problem is to halve the answer (e.g. 20) and check that the result is the previous number in the sequence.

25 20, 160 and 320 should be circled

> Your child should be able to recognise that only numbers that end in 0 are exactly divisible by 10.

26 John's guess of 38 is the nearest

> Being able to recognise the number nearest to a ten is a skill that children may find difficult. Encourage your child to look at the difference between each of the guesses (38 and 44) and 40. The smallest difference is the closer.
> i.e. $40 - 38 = 2 \quad 44 - 40 = 4$

27 £1.25 *or* 125p

> Show your child that this problem can be solved in a couple of ways.
> Multiplication: $25 \times 5 = 125$
> *or* repeated addition: $25 + 25 + 25 + 25 + 25 = 100 + 25 = 125$
> (Repeated addition is a useful tool if your child is not confident with multiplication tables.)

28 4

> Your child needs to know that £1 is the same as 100p.
> Repeated subtraction is one method you could show your child.
> $100p - 25 \Rightarrow 75p - 25 \Rightarrow 50p - 25 \Rightarrow 25p - 25 \Rightarrow 0$
> How many sums? 4.

29 44

> Show your child how addition and subtraction operations can help solve number problems.
> $56 + ? = 100$ can be solved by $100 - 56 = ?$

30 2

> Encourage your child to sort this sum and make it more friendly.
> Find the answer to one side of the problem (i.e. $40 \div 10 = 4$). This will make the problem $? \times 2 = 4$ which is easier to solve.

31 (a) 12   (b) 6   (c) 8

> This pictogram has one circle for 4 children. Remind your child of the importance of looking at the key. You could give more practice by asking what the answers would have been if the circle had represented 2 children, 8 children etc.

32 Two numbers which total 17

> Show your child how to sort this sum to simplify it.
> The answer is 217, you already have 200 which means you need to find two numbers which total 17.

Marking grid

Test A	
1	
2	
3	
4	
5	
6	
7	
8	
9	
10	
11	
12	
13	
14(a)	
14(b)	
15	
16	
17	
18	
19	
20	
21	
22	
23	
24(a)	
24(b)	
25(a)	
25(b)	
25(c)	
26	
27	
28	
29	
30	
31	
32	

Total marks

Test B	
1	
2	
3	
4	
5	
6	
7	
8	
9	
10	
11	
12	
13	
14(a)	
14(b)	
15	
16	
17	
18	
19	
20	
21	
22	
23	
24(a)	
24(b)	
25	
26	
27	
28	
29	
30	
31	
32(a)	
32(b)	
32(c)	

Total marks

Test C	
1	
2	
3	
4	
5	
6	
7	
8(a)	
8(b)	
9	
10	
11	
12	
13	
14(a)	
14(b)	
15	
16	
17	
18	
19	
20	
21	
22	
23	
24	
25	
26	
27	
28	
29	
30	
31(a)	
31(b)	
31(c)	
32	

Total marks

Mark	Level
5–9	1
10–15	2C
16–22	2B
23–29	2A
30–36	3